A
Road
through
Bushes

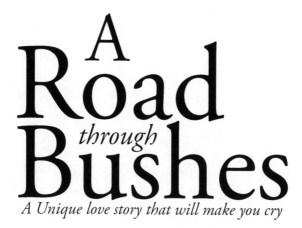

A Road through Bushes

A Unique love story that will make you cry

SHAH ISHTIYAQ MEHFOOZE

PARTRIDGE

A Penguin Random House Company

ISBN: Hardcover   978-1-4828-4489-4
               Softcover   978-1-4828-4488-7
               eBook   978-1-4828-4487-0

Print information available on the last page.

To order additional copies of this book, contact
Partridge India
000 800 10062 62
orders.india@partridgepublishing.com

www.partridgepublishing.com/india

"Dedicated to all lovers world wide"

My deepest sympathies go out to the innocent flowers that lost their lives in the Peshawar school tragedy and the victims of the mighty floods in my beloved Kashmir

Contents

Acknowledgement.. 1

Prologue.. 5

1. A glimpse to the present 11

2. A dream to past 18

3. Here the tale goes 27

4. The journey starts as Friends 67

5. The relationship starts With truth 80

6. At Home 104

7. Closeness 144

8. The Electronic Romance................................ 156

9. The phonic lessons.................................... 189

10. The life taking shock 196

Acknowledgement

First of all thanks to almighty Allah who blessed me with such talent, art, courage and patience to write this one for you; I am glad to write this one for all the lovers of the globe, love is common and everyone loves someone which points out this book is for every organism living in this beautiful world. Writing something is never an individual effort, you need a strong contribution of various people around you who become very special to you when they help you to get to your dream and make you worth respect. I have a long list of such people to thank today from the core of my heart who's small or big but valuable efforts became the reason to get this book to you.

My Family:- My father Ghulam Ahmad Shah and my mother Mehfooza Begum, my grandparents, Abdul Ahad Shah and Mala Begum, My sisters, Sakeena shah, Shaziea shah, Sumeena Shah, Humaira Shah and my brother Aaqib Hussain Shah, thank you for your prayers, sacrifices, suggestions, advices and faith. I can proudly say I have got the most loving parents ever and I am sorry for my stupid mistakes.

Shaziea Wani: - My inspiration. Believe me; I have never seen such incredible, supportive, kind, gentle, beautiful and loving individual in my whole life, thank you for your company, prayers, suggestions and the valuable time you sacrificed for me. I wouldn't have been able even to think about writing if you wouldn't have met me. You made me what I am today. I promise I will never let you go out of my heart. I am always with you now and forever. I love you.

Antoniet Saints:-My publishing consultant for being so humble, kind and responsive. And I thank all the Partridge family for the interest they have shown in me; I again thank them for working with me.

My Teachers:- Teachers are those knowledge factories which builds the respect and recognition of not only an individual but the country as a whole, it would be absolute injustice if I would avoid to send my gratitude to the following people who turned me around. I thank Dr. Dost Muhammad, Dr. Santosh Sharma, Dr. Parveez Abdullah, Mr. Abdul Ahad Baba, Mr. Maqbool Kumar, Mr. Sunil Kumar, Mr. Mohammad Nadim Khan, Dr.. Sampath, Mr. R.R. Srivastava, Miss Akhela, Mrs. Rajini Balaji, Mr. Ghulam Ahmad Shah, Mrs. Nelima Kumari, Mrs. Shriya, Mr. K.Y. Reddy, I again thank you for teaching us your hearts out and making us worth living.

My Friends: - These persons are as important in your life as your heart is, they accompany you everywhere you go and today I have got some sweet time for these people.

Umar Ahanger: - My deepest respect goes out to this guy who supported me financially. Your dreams would always find its way to the skies if you have got such humble, honest and gentle friend in the hunt. I love you.

Mohammad Saleem: - Not only my friend but my teacher as well who guided me at every point of my life, The first person who suggested me to write a book after seeing there was something in me, thank you for your contributions towards making me, what I am today. I am glad to have you by my side.

Ishfaq Malik: - It would be complete injustice not thanking this guy who left his room open every time for me and created an environment for me to write with efficiency.

Not only this, he always remained advising me what to do next. Thank you for your humbleness and placid approach. I would never forget you.

Dr. Kailash Nagar: - The doctor who remained and felt proud to help me when needed and gave nice complements after reading the manuscript, thanks for you kind help.

Jahangeer Ahmad: - The one who always addressed my novel to be among the super hits when it was yet to get completed thank you for the help when it was needed the most.

Anees Hussain: - The healthiest guy, thank you for giving me the best choices for the publication.

Rayees Mir: - The cute little angel who always gave me confidence that I can do it and would tell some of the success stories which boosted me to work even harder, thank you my rabbit. I love you.

Aishwini Kumar: - Since we never met but the advices over the phone proved a lot of difference at the end, thank you for that.

Shafqat Mir: - The person who cracked humorous jokes to feel me relaxed after the huge workload thank you for your small but valuable efforts.

Sushmita Kumari: - The person who let me down at the point when she was needed the most. Thank you for not believing me and thank you for what you did to me, Such incredible human who even let me know what life is all about, but unfortunately I don't know why some people fall around.

Zahoor Mir: - He woke me up to make me worth respect. Thank you for your timely advice.

Aasif Wani: - The comedian and the vast hearted chum thank you for the time you spent with me to make it a memorable journey.

Suhail Dar: - The religious fellow and it was enough powerful what he did for me that was the prayers. Thank you for that.

Prologue

Destinies do almost depend on fate; if she would had been here with us then we might not had got him passing such terrible conditions. His age is going down the ground, we have done a mess, a full family got devastated, and I do declare ourselves demolishers, no doubt we axed him, if we would had excepted what he wanted our son would have been different and happy with his life. Glancing throw the giant door at its threshold slightly open I could see my mother sitting in front of my father sharing these words, precisely I got I am the topic in discussion.

Have to put effortless efforts to get him married, if I go to the other side of the book I may find he opposing all what we wish as usual he does, my mom said diving in depth.

He must be thinking of marriage as well, not only we as he himself signals of being a victim of the same stress. But our worries ultimately had an end now; I have rummaged around a girl who suits him best. He would be happy to know about her profession and the age factor, she is nearly born one year earlier than him which is not a big gap and above all it is a diamond opportunity for him to get life partners with her, only thirty six, and a lawyer. A handy profession!

Has she never married or there is any other reason for her to be single yet? My mom asked a genuine question.

Not any uncommon reasons besides a divorce two years earlier, even the percentage of divorces is elevating in our country and it is a bad sign, anyway she is a divorcee and has a daughter of eight who is being fed by her father.

Sam is not going to marry her and that is for sure. My mom said and I could see her wiping her eyes indicating if she wanted to quit the discussion.

We are not going to tell him all about this; it's a golden opportunity for him I expect you not to make a mistake by telling him all about that girl, if you do, tell everything except the divorce case, my father said in a little louder voice.

Can't we find another one for him, a girl without marriage? How long will it remain a secret? If not this but someday he would come to know his parents had cheated him. My mom said in a gentle tone adjusting the sari on her head.

Do you think a girl of her age would be still a bachelor? You should think he is thirty five and more over he is being rejecting marriages since years.

My eyes cannot see him suffering like this; he is the light of my eyes, my GOD what happened to my son, my mom said crying and I put my eyes off her face, I couldn't bear her sobbing.

Let him come from the hospital, he will be asked to get ready to visit her house to see if they can start a new life together, my father said.

Its 12th September today and he will be going some unique place to celebrate his birthday as he usually does. Once I heard that sentence from my mother it again proves that an only mother cares everything about her child.

What happened? My father said.

It's his birthday; he will be going to some place to celebrate it as usual. My mother again said the same words.

I will also attach not to go there as her family has to move for a trip by tomorrow evening itself. My father said enough confidently to get me married this time.

My mother looked down, and pulled her head up to put a word to my father saying, "I don't know why I feel our family is vanished, will Sam forgive us ever?" Not the question but how it was asked broke me copiously. How many of you can see your mother crying over your name and you are there watching without wiping her eyes? No one, yeah! But if there is someone it is me. I got hurt for my own; it was none of their faults and above all no one wants to blame his parents.

You don't worry I will get it to be right in some time, my father said.

My eyes never want to see him in worse situation behaving if nothing had happened. We people need to validate our perceptions and we need to drain out the conservatism, it is hazardous, we got a proof already. I never found any fault what he told that day. I accept his career was more important that time but we should have considered his case later. We are the guiltiest and we know it. We can't eat up the story; the newer generations wouldn't be so obeying and would never accept his case when the vagabonds of their generations would get married even easier as per their wishes. My mother cried out some genuine points.

Yeah! We should get him married now, my father said.

Don't think he would accept, said my mother.

We will try to convince and motivate him the most awful experience I experienced was learning a lesson from getting the marriage fixed for decades is a hell of ideas, many people practiced this but it went vicious for us, we made it enough mess by fixing his marriage with her cousin sister only hours after his birth when most of the people were yet to get his gender. My father said.

Anyway it is nice to have one more chance for him, my mother said emotionally.

In Indian villages a thirty five year old lady is approximately a grandmother and it applies in the cases of males too, I find it difficult to search a girl for him and I think she best suits him. My father said.

The environment outside was boring enough and meanwhile the wind starts blowing over. The door starts moving to and fro screeching every window and every door rattle by the pace of the blowing air, the house was already very big and as per modernity it was the most liked and desired house with complete fifteen bedrooms and half dozen bathrooms with first class ventilation constructed as a gift for whom it proves to be a never come true dream to live here together.

I could see father trying to speak up some extra and he does----Probably we could have seen him happy with her wife and children, he replied into a pitying gentle tone.

And one could always see tears rolling down my cheeks when anyone would discuss about her. It was ten or fifteen minutes after I came from her grave praying for her life to be in high spirits into the heavens and begging her to forgive me for what I can't did for her. I stood dumb near the threshold, listening all what they could share, yeah they were very much poignant over what they did. I went off that place and opted to close all windows and doors of the house as the wind increased its speed. I pulled out the last letter she gave me and start reading the saddest lines ever.

It was quiet unexpected to think to do something after reading the emotional lines except to put the face into both of the palms and tears finding their ways to get your hands soaked. I dived on the bed pulled the towel and masked my face after lying chest upwards. I don't know what time is but I only know it is a thing which made even the storms my friend then now the equation is I am myself not a friend to me.

Luckily I put that thought away before damaging my eyes further, washed my face and went to my parents' room acting if I know nothing of their discussion. I greeted them before my right foot got inside and hugged my mom tightly but unfortunately our hearts fall to the opposite sides.

My sweet mother, my darling, what is special tomorrow? Can you guess? I put a question to her just to make her feel better.

How can I forget it is you birthday my loving son and note you are not going away to celebrate it, let's do it here. She said.

Na na na na na na ….. I can't. I can't chop the promises. At least I can do these little things for her; so that her soul may get a little comfort, I cannot produce myself anymore a coward. I was made to avoid her when she did every impossible thing for me now everybody wants her when they know she can't even cry my name. I said hugging my mother tighter once again.

What do you want my son? She said seeing deep into my eyes very emotionally.

Nothing, my mom, just let me to go out for tomorrow. People have their wives, daughters, sons, sisters and brothers to gossip around on such occasions, I have no one except the things she left with me.

1

A glimpse to the present

After listening my parent's discussion over my marriage, it is out of question to stay at my home today no matter what the circumstances are. I think all over my body is the date "13ᵗʰ September" embedded the day which is so special for me perhaps the odd one for some other. I can forget my meals but this date? Never! It was sharp thirty five years ago when I was born to a strict father and a very loving mother. A father who would always try to find faults in you and a mother who would always sacrifice her meals when I wasn't at home, I think you came to the point that my mother was more associated with me than my father and she loved to stay with me keeping eyes into eyes for longer times.

13ᵗʰ September, aha! A day of double happiness, apart from my birthday I found my true love right on this day fine 18 years ago. Yeah! I am 35 but please don't question, I will tell you the whole story.

My birthday hasn't a definite spot to be celebrated at every year I would go to different tourist places of my beautiful

Kashmir to have it with no one around me and this day I decided to visit Gulmarg, a world famous tourist place but very memorable for me as well. I knew my day will pass like an owl flying during the day time without knowing which way to go hence gets struck to the things coming its way. Everybody knows about the beauty and charm of this place, it became the most visited tourist places in Kashmir. I bowed my head to get into the vehicle to get me there. Gulmarg look superb and the breeze had some unique fragrance into it. I could see couples taking pleasure of horse riding; the fountains and the immense meadows seem changed very much since I was here some years before. All it is love from each corner but seeing by my side I never found it with me like it was before. Yeah! Such a special day and I found no one to share with me, neither my beloved nor my children, not five or six but I think one or two would have been enough, but no. I had come here with my feelings and I am sure they will never let me go down, I trust them. I walked fifties of times up and down the landscapes but I never enjoyed, no matter how the beauty I see or taste. I could see a couple pointing towards me saying this man is alone and is involved in the depth of his thoughts, a bitter reality.

How can I be so alone? A man of thirty five without her wife and children has come to such a place to spend his thirty fifth birthday addressing it as a part of his past memories. I am not any Salman Khan who is surrounded by indifference curves, don't be confused it's very simple, I mean I am not him who is surrounded my millions of beautiful ladies and is still puzzled whom to choose as his wife. I am a simple man a doctor by profession who wants neither to marry nor to survive. I am waiting when death would knock my door but it never come. I wondered here and there but never find the joy and happiness like it was when we both met here some twelve years ago.

The sun is going to the westwards, and the breeze extends, all the tourists opened their lunch boxes and start having their meals, but I starred them. I was left with nothing except my past memories. A gentle man called me to have lunch with them and I replied negatively by thanking them.

I sat on the never ending green carpet which adds the beauty, the breeze extends its speed and the trees start moving and dropping yellowish leaves on the grassy surface. The sun was at maximum warmth and I choose a tree to lie down under.

Your emotions get increased when you start visiting a place like this, the nature wants you to think over it but your tragedy dominates it. I am totally a changed and reduced man now, unlike ten years before I would like to go to such places only to bring inspiration into me and immediately change them into romantic and natural poems, romantic ones would go to her as gifts and natural to nature. But things had been changed for me now; it is all emotions I would get from any couple falling in love. This word came with a disaster in my life; I always link this word with pain, destruction, and sorrows plus feeling pity over the love birds cause I always think how many of them would succeed and how many would get pains and sorrows as rewards and how many would commit suicide and how many will naturally demise before they get married, this was all my mind was packed with.

Deep into my thoughts I could hear someone greeting me like he was my old chum; I turned around and saw a man with hardly any facial skin visible dressed like if he works here, I put my thought away and looked into his eyes to recognize him and succeeded.

Sam, he discovered me.

Yeah? Oh! Hoo! I know you, isn't that horse yours? My dear how are you? You look a man now. I said. I hugged him after and I tapped him followed asking about his health.

Don't bother about me sir, I am fine, you completed your doctoral?

Yeah! Brother, I replied in a simplest way.

And your Saba, where is she. He said and I ignored to reply.

Hoch! You had got a long beard, how could you be known, the small boy with the blue eyes, you where then. I tried to put his question away.

Call your Saba and children; let's have some riding over there, he exclaimed.

How could you say I am married, I am not, I said in a pitying tone.

Don't be so witty now, please, this one is free for you, he swears.

Oh my dear, don't be so vigorous, I said pointing towards him.

I want your children and Saba, I will do some favor for you today.

I am alone here, she hasn't come with me, nor my children, today I had planned to finish this day without them, to confirm how it feels, I explained if she had married me, and I had ignored her today, totally opposite, you would know.

But why so, He asked for, if he was my father, enough orderly.

I noticed he was getting panic; he was not any acquaintance but my school friend who hated to study.

He knew something was wrong but in his opinion a professional person would always succeed in these matters, not they have some magic but for the reason being the first choice in front of those parents who are not much educated although managed to pocket in a mini government job. He wants to know the story but struggled to say to explain it to him.

I got some emotions and so did he without awareness about the story, yeah! He never had.

It was very late now, I requested him to go and earn his wages, and the tourists will no longer be here, don't you know Ramadan is approaching.

Shit to that tourists, and don't bother I usually do some other work in the month of blessings, he discerned to tell him the problem, it appears he was very sad, I thought he was feeling very sympathetic for we too without knowing anything.

You dude, why you are so emotional, I said in a tender mode.

Dear brother, it's too late you need to reach Kupwara and don't forget you are at such a place where from you need to change four five vehicles to reach your home, I think you can't, so come with me to my home; he said in an old fashioned hospitability way.

No I have my own car, I can easily go, and I will run very fast, my mother would be waiting me.

Come to my poor house, at least I can serve you my best.

Hey! How can you think such harsh about me, I really love you, you were my sole friend whom I had shared my secrets with, remember? And note no matter how great I and you are we have to forever afar and that is common to all. Until we have to share the same world under the same roof. Even the political laws and the laws of nature are same for us. You are my best friend for me it's hard to forget those who made my past much wonderful by sacrificing whatever they had; even your footprints are there over my heart. And don't think cheap, we are friends to each other no need to be formal with me. And do utter whatever you like but not when you would come to my clinic to get medicine, we both laughed.

I also know the honor and the brotherhood you paid me, you really let your footprints over my heart, but I think you should stay with me this night, will recover our days and will have lots of fun. He stepped further.

But how would he know the conditions I am living in, let me to speak him the truth, no it will take time I am getting late, I thought into my inner, anyway I never want him to feel sad.

What say? Sam.........

Huh, I prefer to go home, mom and dad are alone, hope I will meet you soon, I concluded.

Ok, but take a little gift for your wife, she will look dashing after wearing it, he said after he forwarded me a typical Kashmir shawl.

Thank you, I said.

Never mention, he said.

He greatly astounded me. I kept mum and did hurry to escape before I fall into that thought again. I became frigid inside again.

My phone rang, a typical Nokia tone, Oh! It is mom calling as the name flashed on the screen.

Hello, my son where are you, it's getting late, and you know the condition of our state, she told a bit faster and surprised.

Yeah! Mom I would be there after two hours, I guarantee and I hung up quickly before she could scold me.

Ok, my bro, good night, stay blessed, I went to shake hands with him but he hugged me very tightly.

I raced my car as fast as I could and reached home after one hundred twenty eight minutes, thanks to my guessing power.

I greeted my mom before I entered my home she responded giving me a lovely slap followed by a beautiful hug.

You hadn't given it away yet, the late night roaming. She said caringly.

Mom I am fine, I just met my friend being cause to late, ok my life I am sorry, please forgive me now, and I swear not to commit it again, I begged her, not for I was sorry for my mistake but for the love and care that was still for me in her eyes. She had already a desire to see me married before she would leave me here. She always craved to see my children laughing and moving in her arms but what would I do, would I prefer to keep my promise alive till my death or would I fulfill mothers desire, these are the two things that are responsible to eat my flesh every day. What shall I do?

I gave full attention towards the dinner and went to my room to have a sleep.

2

A dream to past

I have never seen such beauty in my lifetime the air blowing such graciously welcoming me over such a wonderful place, where I am? What am I watching? I don't know. The tulips, the marigolds, the Lilly and the roses attracted my eyes to be focused on them. The breeze would drop them either way and they would bow at some moments, looks if they are offering a prayer. The fruit trees on the other hand would let your mouth to dribble by showing their red, pink, tasty, and enormous existence on the shaggy dense trees with evergreen leaves the branches of which are kissing the green surface making an umbrella structure. It is what my eyes hadn't seen during these thirty-five odd years. I wonder who has left such garden open; anyone could break into to take advantage. The grass beneath looked if a thin green never ending woolen carpet is mushroomed all the way, for weeds I swear I never found one. I looked above; the sky seemed was never there, the different and colorful species of birds moving here and there were found not getting into gluttony to impair or to fed on the shining fruits and that was the wonderful difference I observed between these birds and the birds I have seen till yet. As I walked deep into the garden its beauty got bloated and beauty got bloated and its compactness went denser. Who was I? Can anybody tell me and where am I? How I came here? Who lives here? Who has maintained this all? My mind got occupied with these questions and there was nobody to answer. Prior getting there I had seen only water flowing from canals, but I got faint on seeing the canals filled with milk. The air had an exceptional flavor, not an average sixteen kilograms, but a normal man could inhale as much air equaling to his weight per day. The leaves were full of juice and the trees would produce outsized sap all I could see around that made me feel if I was residing into a heaven and wanted to imbibe all the physical things amusing me inside since a long time but somewhat I feel sacred of doing that after the mighty colorful lights went functional simply promised if the sun lives here insisting me to forget everything to get stayed here as I could see a mound of colorful lights towering some thirty feet above the ground extended triangularly approximately twenty feet wide marveled me to my full and I perceived it to be some other magical prospect but was proven wrong when getting it to be an oversized golden house decorated in such a way that no one could stop it from being voted as the number one wonder of the world of the modern era moreover I couldn't see anything which would give me a clue that somebody lives here and all I did was to start getting carved inside to consume all what I had seen till yet to take the pleasure of such innovative and wonderful things of which my eyes haven't the pleasure to be gazed at through my entire life anyway I made myself to knock the door twinkling like a star and glittering like a gold I moved out lacking courage even to touch it and could see only colorful lights instead the timber and all its parts were glittering but I tried to sum up some guts to knock it before I could hear.

"My life, my darling" go in, you don't need anybody's permission to get into your own home; you already took much time to come back, keep the fruits in the basket and come back.

Ghaaassshuuuuu (the light of my eyes)........I screamed the lovable name as louder as my throat could produce.... Is it my sweetheart? Yeah! It was her. I glanced here and there and found no one, where from the voice came I didn't know, I remain dumbstruck to reply. I rotated my neck approx 180 degrees and found a lady playing with cute children three in number. No precincts for my joy to go jumping towards her. It was my Saba.

My life...my sweetheart...where were you for these years, I embraced her and my eyes couldn't stop to be mum this time, wasn't I missing you my darling? I sobbed with eyes red and gazing her.

Hahahahaha...what happened. She said.

My life, you don't know how I have managed to spend rest of my life without you; I simply want to broke into your heart to stay there till the Day of Judgment.

Oh! Hoo! I know you are my life, my husband and everything tell me what happened.

She behaved if she was with me all time, I was mad to get her single glimpse and she is taking all this lightly which I hadn't expected to happen. All the cute children start starling me.

No more joking, I know you are good in acting, did you kept the fruits in the kitchen? She asked.

What acting, what fruits and what kitchen, I want to know each answer, are you all right, why are you letting me down, isn't there any respect for me into your heart, have you forgot who I am?

That is what I need to ask you, you went to bring some fruits from the garden some minutes before that is it. How can I disrespect a person who is my breeze? Please don't say like this.

Leave it all. Let's go to our village, I will introduce you with my family and you don't have any idea how happy they would be to get that I have married with a girl for whom even the walls of my home wanted her to be there to make my soul meaningful, come, come.

Oh! I am not getting what you are asking. What is it? Where is the question of going to the village if we are living here since years? I don't know any village you just lay down I will check if you had any problem, she said.

Who are they? I pointed towards the cute children.

Forgot? How can it happen? Aren't they our children? How can you forget, her tone and body gestures changed after I asked the question, she looked worried, enough worried.

But I never know them, have you married? I asked.

Oh! My GOD, what type of question is this; they are our children, the apple of our eyes. She explained.

To whom you had married. I asked.

I still don't know is it a comedy or a serious display from you, nobody falls ill here it's not me but the sayings of GOD, which reflects it is nothing other a comedy from your creative mind. Keep doing, I don't care. It's enough now, we had married some nine years ago and please get this comedy closed.

No, I am unmarried. You just show me a picture of the person whom you have married.

She clasped my hand and showed a landscape hanging by the wall in that house.

It's me, I shouted. I am seeing you after several years, how could you marry me. No alternative except to gaze around, I almost went mad thinking of the issue. I wanted to know what all this was, but the person who could explain me was herself caught into the same mystery. I came closer to the portrait run my hands over it, I looked around, I haven't seen such wonderful house in my life, there was no scarcity of anything, calmness everywhere, the canals flowing milk through them stunned and faded in me Saba is any normal individual now. She clung on my wrist to get me into the park again, she called the little cute children to sit beside their father, and obviously I was not.

Papa, papa, what happened to you dear papa? Why you don't identify our mom, will you leave us alone here? A cute little child jumped into my lap and spoke the touching lines, how can it happen a child knows his father when his father is yet to get married? I involved myself into a deep thought gazing Saba and the cute children.

Trin..trin…trin…trin…trin…trin…trin…Oh!   My GOD… Sam, it's late to your hospital, come on, your phone is ringing also… some noisy loud voices and the phone could be heard ringing all at once… it produced a chunky obnoxious sound to my ears, its already eight, get up! Get up! Get ready!

Where I am? And what was it all? I questioned myself. My mind and heart coordinated and gave me the answer. That opened my eyes and I wondered where and what I was doing. My heart broke into pieces knowing it was a dream, I was crushed and my knees seem getting weaker, there was no life in me, the soul had gone. I buried my head into the palms to get a handful of tears. My Sweetie you aren't here? The only sentence I could manage to say. My dream got shattered just like my life has been since past couple of years.

What would happen further in my life, the dream conveyed me all that, my parents do have a plan to get me married but no, I can't, it's the first time I found myself married, Saba has already married me in the heavens, I don't know but she lives with me each and every second. I had never seen such Saba whom I see tonight, so happy and wealthy, what to ask more to GOD to give. I don't know why I feel I am alone; she lives with me and with her cute children happily at such a place where even billionaires can't reach. GOD has given her a gift for her sufferings and sacrifices she had went through for my sake.

The dream came up with the message, Sam your Saba is waiting you in the heavens land, It is sure to get a better life after I sleep forever, I would thank GOD before I would feel I am dying. Death is uncertain, so was our reunion. I knew now the moment I would demise I would meet my beloved. How far could I wait, shall I commit suicide to get to meet Saba, yeah it is an option to leave this miserable world as soon as possible to spend the prosperous life with my Saba but no, that was not the way, it's an offence not only in the government laws but in the laws of almighty as well. I can't get my reward if I did so, let's wait the time to come, it may be, one day, two days, ten years or so, death is sure and uncertain.

It was better to put that panic thought away to get ready for the hospital, I want to sleep to get the dream back to see that person again and again who has sacrificed her every right for my sake but alas! The dream can't be dreamed once it is crushed, the time is gone. With eyes red and still producing tears I started to get ready for the hospital with my knees totally broken. I got myself ready in no time and rushed into my car without any breakfast.

The shape and the surrounds of the hospital was dull and gloomy, the cries and the wail forced my legs to cross the threshold slowly. The pain bearing trait in me has gone long way, I cannot never. As soon as I reached the hospital, the panic cries uncomfortable for both my ears and soul got heavier, people were visible rushing in and out of the main door punching their chests in poignancy. The ladies with the confused hair could be heard grumbling against lord's name, I was perplexed what to do next. I guess it was a serious case.

Being a doctor the courage in me was nowhere, I went directly in the emergency hall to see what had actually happened, an approximate twenty one year old boy was seen vomiting and his mouth do produce a lot of foam; the strong diagnostic power helped me know it was a suicidal attempt.

Had he taken any poison? I said a lady besides him.

Yes sir! Rat killer, she replied.

A team of doctors was already there.

The foam was coming out continuously and he was struggling to breathe, soon we implemented our profession and knowledge and skill and put activated charcoal into business to avoid the poison to get absorbed into the blood further and a ventilator to get his breathing smooth. A toxicology screen test was performed including a liver functioning test which came normal now. Thanks to him for taking this otherwise he would have gone if he had tried some other strong one.

He was found normal after some hours and I tried to find out the cause of his poisoning, as his mother had told me to do so.

Hi boss! As I forward my hand to him.

Yes sir! He gave his hand to me slowly with his head down.

What happened to you my dear, what made you to do this, I asked him.

Nothing sir! He tried to quit.

See, even I have gone through this stage and I can guess correctly, I know what the cause is but I wanted it to hear from you. Don't be any shy or formal, I promise your case would be considered. I said.

He understood what I said and went directly to the cause.

He started his cause like a philosophy professor and went like this;

"Sir, my name is Farad an engineering student of semester eight. I wouldn't say I should have not done what I did, I really forgot everyone around me for my beloved whom I love a lot. I had never thought our love life would take such a curve where we had only a single option to die once or to die million times if opted to survive. Though it is India, the country where love marriages rarely took place and moreover a girl is considered mature for marriage when she had hardly crossed twenty or may be twenty one or something lesser that that. Her parents are very conservative and narrow minded they caught her red handed while talking with me, and without asking anything they are going to get her married soon to a man of thirty two. I stood totally dumb when she called me to say this. I couldn't answer nor reply her. Four days passed when she verbalized to elope unfortunately she was not allowed to go outside forcing me to try this option. Second there was not ever a paisa in my pocket and being the only son in six sisters was the biggest hurdle into my ways. I really can't do that, but if I would go to avoid this then I had to sacrifice my love, and if I would elope, I had to sacrifice my parents and my innocent sisters, how can I leave my parents into the hell for generations to come and how can I water their dreams and mine. She would get married in few months if I couldn't do anything and my life will be shattered forever. Sir, I can't even think to live without her. I don't know what to do before opting to leave her forever".

I understood his story to full with great interest, my eyes showed some emotions for him, I could know the value of his dropping tears, I tried to hide mine, it was a story exact to mine, and I would say my story was the mother of his story. Soon I looked into his eyes and run my hand through his hairs lovingly and gently.

Hey! Dude, why are you so puzzled? I said him.

Nothing is out of your ways I will help you I promised.

Why you saved me doctor, I want to die. He starts crying.

I saved you because I know your girl is waiting you to become the source of her happiness forever. What do you think I am a normal like others? I questioned.

Not at all, but Yeah! Sir, the girl who had married you is a lucky one. He answered in a jiffy. Your kindness and the humanity you had simply make you great.

How much you love her? I asked him.

More than anything in this world, he gave a wise answer.

You are able to see or talk her?

Yes sir! Off course, why not?

What about a man you love her beloved more than himself but have never seen her since a decade? I questioned.

Tragedy sir! It is an exceptional case and I want to know the story sir. Please.

No, no, I will pray you but I can't tell you that story, it's very emotional and it would take time.

Please sir!

You can't bear and even I can't tell my own story.

Is it your story? He was shocked.

Yes my dear. It is my story.

He pleads to tell him that, I agreed.

Would tell you after your promise that you would not cry, if you did, I would stop telling. I acquaint him with some smile on my face.

Ok, sir I will not he answered.

It was not important to touch this topic but I feel it to be known to everyone so that they may learn how to cope up with hard times in their life. I like to hear and tell stories but it is the first time I am telling you what is my reason to live.

Listen to me now and be ready to sit still for next three hours, I smiled and warned him.

3

Here the tale goes

As soon as I made myself prepared to tell him my story, everything seemed to change as it was then, I found myself if I was changing into a kid of twelve, a sixth class student, the sky for me changed much cloudy and the breeze starts to do its job, yeah! I could find myself at the base of the story some twenty three years ago. The environment changed for me as it was then as the land changed into open meadows and became less denser the nights presented much murky and the water bodies increased in the number. The population becomes thinner the males were visible wearing long pajamas and the females were seen totally masked only the eyes and some part of face visible. I could hear the sweet existence of the dogwoods in the landscapes. I found my nose wet for the major part of the day, my height suddenly decreased from five point nine inch to some four, my development reduced as my face looked much fleshy and creamy without any plantation on it, my thinking and mental strength got diminished. I found my legs and arms going thin and shiny, the depth of my voice also decreased. I could find the construction diminishes and the roads got narrower with lots of trees and plants planted around, the oriental plane trees got increased and the ground got much fired up with the glimpse of the unlimited leaves over it making a cracking sound when crushed, perhaps they were crying not to break them apart. The springs changed into more natural a hub of thousands of fishes and other aquatic creatures, the fountains shoot the water very high like the gun shots, the trees become more dense and widespread with green bases. The fields were harvested and every household seemed happy what they got. The little girls appeared collecting the leaves and twigs of the trees for fuel in the upcoming winter. Everyone seemed happy, including the animals and birds as they got much to eat and much plants and trees to make their shelter into. I could see the nature on its top; Kashmir had fewer infrastructures but was blessed with the nature beauty immensely. By setting my eyes on the entire environment I remembered Dr. Sir Muhammad Iqbal, commonly known as the poet of the east, had once said if there is heaven on earth it is here it is here it is here. I went to see myself into the mirror which showed my hair an inch long, oiled unlike before so I thought to lay down for some minutes before I could go to the playground. The whistle rang immediately after I planned this, it was our sports captain, whistling and warning everyone not to stay into their dormitories without any cause. It was Jawahar Novodaya Vidyala my first boarding school in Lolab valley accurate a dozen kilometers away from my home. Lolab, very famous for its water resources, natural beauty and the dense forests, it is the hub of different wild beasts as well and the poet of east had made it the main source of his legendary poetry. People would come from corners of the world to tang the real nature phenomenon here. Children's also liked this place from the core of their hearts and schools from each part of Kashmir would come here for Excursion.

I hardly forget the days and dates and this one was on the tip of my tongue *Saturday, 19 October 1991.* It not only completed our two months in the boarding school but the mess menu showed it was chicken in the dinner making the day a special one to remember and in hostels such days are respected and being waited restlessly through the entire week. And second reason of its specialty was Saturday itself, the happiest day throughout the week followed by Sunday, fun day. I was quiet confident that every student would take bulk of pleasure from the feast in the evening. This school is the sign of intelligence and excellence and some schools do visit here not for its site but to see the innocent intelligent faces that made their way here after passing the hardest entrance test.

It's your village school visiting here today, they had gone to Sogam, but they will visit our school also, one of my friends was shouting in delight referring to me.

Who told you this? I said.

Principal Sir, he answered.

My ears could hear, *"Sam today you may get to see the beautiful angles of your village and please do select a stoutest one with big eyes"* it was my one of the seniors.

He was yet to complete his sentence when an identical queue of girls was seen entering the main gate, some hundreds teeny heights with petite faces where visible with their heads moving like a pendulum perhaps catching the glimpse of this school first time. Their similar dresses and tiny steps reminds me the ants when they use to go out to collect the foodstuff for the winter, the difference was only their dresses, this queue had got a whitish look but the ants either black or red.

I don't think boys could ever stop commenting on girls especially the hostellers who always stay waiting such moments like hungry loins, they are capable of hunting but never get to find a prey; if they could I am sure the prey would never want to exist again. Boys always go on watching all the fuss a girl is having from top to bottom either it is front, left, right and backwards, this was the reason the senior boys were whistled back to their corridors when the school rested in the playground for some time before they could take a sight of the whole campus.

The juniors below eighth standard had no restrictions as they carried on with the games they were playing.

The juniors start interacting with the girls and I was rummaging around for someone from my village. It feels very good and commiserative when somebody from your village or region visit the place where you spend your life according to the tenants laid and inferior working under others. Jawahar Novodaya Vidyalayas' were among those schools where students are bound to study hard without their parents and doing all the fuss for them by them. For some students these types of schools are only meant for heart attacks alike the prisons. It is not like Jawahar Novodaya's aren't the best schools in the entire India but it is the fact that to go only a day absent from your home for educational purposes seems centuries but going there for centuries for some other purpose seems like a day. That was the only reason students call these boarding schools with another name *'prisons'*.

I start looking very deeper to the girls after reading the name of the school the reason being my cousin sister was a student of the same school, after some five or six minutes I saw a group of girls coming towards me, and at the centre I discovered her bold enough and perhaps getting more virtuous to find me there.

I was very happy when I saw her with the sexy force as boys usually does after getting beauty in bulk not only this but their eyes roam around on every face and building some romantic scenes inside, and their choices gets broaden which one to choose to be the prey. She greeted me and me too, I shake hands with her and with her friends too before she introduced me to them. They all went happy and smiling to have some chat; my cousin sister holds my right hand to sit down.

Boys or girls are very tiny to think of any attraction of the opposite gender when they are yet to pass their sixth standard but I was an exception I hadn't much time to see everyone's faces during the conversation but I believe beautiful faces always invite everyone's eyes to look at them and your heart and mind are so active to start building romantic buildings which never gets completed but complicated. It was not like that there wasn't any such face going to be the prey to my eyes, yeah a girl in them, quiet shy, beautiful and simple start attracting my eyeballs to be focused on her continuously after sitting under the giant popular tree. I observed her through my eye corner twenty plus times and each time I saw her looking downwards with her eyes focused onto the ground providing a golden chance for me to visit all of her body in installments so that it couldn't be sighted out what I was doing. The first view I took on her showed me her face, cheeks and other beautiful thing beneath her fascinate nose, shiny lips were they, quiet red promising to have a good amount of blood into her body and in the another attempt I went to see her body beneath her neck and so on till my third eye found me climbing to the Mount Everest with esteem speed. It would be wrong to say that I took appropriate advantage of her shyness, keeping her head down was the biggest mistake she had done because in-front of me it was just like playing in the power play with none of the fielders into the ground. I was very delighted to take full benefit of the power play, I noticed her from every corner and she looked simplest and beautiful among all, I forgot everything and found myself into her heart for a while, she was very beautiful inside. I started liking her very much I wished to be with her all time to talk with her and to take visions of her exquisite face. I don't know how to baptize it, should I name it a love or something else but at that age if I would tell someone that I was in love I was sure he would have declared me a scalawag or ne'er-do-well or anything like that, but I myself couldn't know it was really a hearty heartily magnetism which is called love. I know you are smiling but don't feel confused I was in love at the first sight. I don't know why I felt like all my joys and sorrows were reduced by fifty percent and the world look mine now, no enemies and no sorrows. Was it a magic that my heart looked more confident now, I don't know. It looks like the sun the moon the stars the air the trees and the meadows only works for me and are made for me, to me they look smiling and gesturing victory to me.

We had a lot of chat the time was closer to the evening prayers the stars start showing themselves twinkling and the sun had already gone to light the next half of the earth some hundred minutes ago things start disappearing slowly as the surroundings were being blackly colored. I once again looked to her innocent and clear face but couldn't manage to take my eyes off she was really a masterpiece but I someway managed to say her how are you? And what is your name? Everybody laughed. The sentence which should have been said to her much earlier, the *'I am fine'* and *"my name is Saba wani"* from her innocent mouth was something that touched my heart not for the reason her voice sounded sweet but it was the first chance I had managed to talk with a girl who woke up my romantic feelings for the first time and secondly It was the first time she had focused her eyes into mine during the two hour conversation. Her lips stroke each other letting the pieces of sounds come out and manufacture different meaningful words, *I, am, fine.* I liked it and forced me to widen my lips to its maximum.

With this the whistle rang and we stood up for the roll call and they prepare themselves to walk off after shaking hands with me but hell to their principal sir who screeched at our group before she could put her hands into mine leading her to pull her hand back and I remained seeing my empty one but nothing was lost yet as I wisely start walking behind them so take some vision to her backside.

The time my eyeballs focused her from backside her structure looked if she was a fish, everything was placed at the right place and in the right manner; They got to their bus in no time and before the bus would start all of them weaved their hands in order to say me good bye for the last time. The girl with the magical look saw me last time before she dropped her head down and the look was enough lovely as it added some flavor by the sweet smile she had at last. But I was sure it was not any sign of love from her side she was just saying good bye to such a guy who made them laugh for the entire time and who does all his best to settle her fishy body into his eyes just to dream about all the things his eyes witnessed during the long stay under the giant popular tree.

My mind start thinking about the girl but where from she was I still don't know nor did tell my cousin sister but her name stick the walls of my heart and mind. You need not to memorize the names of such beautiful faces but their names find its place itself into your heart for generations to come, so I think Saba was a good face and that is why her name directly sticks to the walls of my mind.

After some time the bus started and was soon invisible.

How could one stay still when such beautiful girl knocked the door of your heart? I can't, nor can be I; you can't be invisible all the time like this when my heart would go searching you, I need you now, I need all of you to keep myself satisfied this time that time each time every time forever.

Everything changed for me as soon as she became invisible, I start missing something very deeply like I had lost something but I kept that onto a bay. I went to the corridor opened our English book and start reading the famous poem written by Pablo Neruda *"today I can write"*, I found myself missing her much now, but there was not a medicine to cure for that except to recollect her once more.

It wouldn't be wrong to say that she had a much attractive physique with chest outwards at a good height, stomach inwards and so was her back, a big amount of flesh on her hips going either side when she would walk and it was pleasant to hear the jangling after her tiny feet hit the ground. There was nothing to avoid from her body from her hairs to the jangling, her brown straight hair that flew on her face and the way she helped them behind the ears was simply fabulous. Her lips that moved in a unique way while saying *"I am fine"* and *"my name is Saba"* looked like a fish eating something with its tiny mouth. Above all her clothes that fit her body in each and every angle was something that would disturb me during the nights, I was sure.

Our hostel was a newly constructed building but it looked a decade old, everyone knows the youth would never stop writing the nonsense stuff on the walls, not only on the walls of the class rooms but the interrogation is done to every wall whether it is class room, bathroom and toilet rooms. The interrogation elevates in case of toilet rooms where one can find the unreadable stuff with some ghastly dire images. Though I had my own values and I was addressed as the laziest guy in the hostels besides being quick in the cricketing field. Perhaps it was my body structure which helped them to search such a nick name for me. I was very careless about the things as well

I would never mind changing the uniform until the late nights when everyone was about to sleep. I was always late in each and every field if it was going to the mess or going to the doors.

Another horrifying thing regarding me was I used to purchase ten to fifteen pens into a span of seven days not because I write more because I would always forgot where I had placed them as the result I always lost them leaving me no option left to buy another one and this routine repeats again every day. Not only this I was even famous in changing the locks of my trunk because I used to do the same treatment with the keys I does with the pens.

Let the humorous habits be apart I had some of the good habits as well, I never wrote a single word on the walls or one the windows and secondly I never went for a toilet during the class and third one I never used to talk unnecessary in the class to make foolish noises.

But no one ever know that I was a guy of jam-packed romance, their lived another Sam in the gentle lazy Sam, the romantic one who was very attracted to the physique of the girls, precisely yes, but no one was known to that except me myself.

So it was very hard for me to tell that I was in love I was scared as well, I don't know what would their reaction be if I told them about it. I ate up my case and let it to develop into my heart and mind only, I was sure they will make fun of me.

Time passed, more the nights I spend more where the crazy dreams, some were even crazier. One of the crazy dreams was having her besides me with seven sons and four daughters around us which puzzled me because her structure was not so big to give birth to a football team nor will she allow me to do this even if I would make her president of the USA not for "*hum do hamare do*" [we two and our two] campaign but for she always loved her structure and would never want to get it destructed for half of her life.

Nothing changed for next four years there were same dreams and the same thoughts till I passed my matriculation with very low percentage. I was scared to ask my cousin sister about her frequently because she was the girl with whom my marriage was fixed only some seconds after my birth. It is called Indian arranged marriages. A boy or girl is yet to get birth but their marriages are fixed. It is just like a case of sport fixing in sports.

My percentage of marks was constantly going down to earth being the biggest reason that my father got to admit me in other good school in the city side for my higher studies. I never wanted to study rather to find her besides me to write stories and poems about her beauty. There was another battle in my home for the subjects I should choose further, I villages parents never look over the talents of their children but force them to study the giant medical books because by mistake they have heard somewhere these are the books which would make their child a doctor or engineer. There are millions of jobs available to a person but in villages its only three either doctor or engineer if not them then a private teacher. I tried to insist my parents that I wanted to become a writer but they declared me mad. In no to go time I was admitted in Sky Touch Public School Srinagar, a school famous for producing renowned doctors and engineers but I never wanted to be one among them.

I was shocked over my parents decision and I was about to go mad thinking how would I stay there. I know nothing and the science books looks like refrigerators' so big and fat. I never know anything about mathematics, chemistry and biology the subjects I have passed with statues in the metric examination. I was sure I would never pass higher secondary.

We had seven sections in the eleventh grade in the new school as expected I was initially thrown into the section G the last one because my percentage was very poor. The school authorities also warned me if my percentage would go down in this grade as well class they would not accept me for the next grade which adds to my pains.

My initial days were same as they were in my previous school; I was still lazy with myself.

The girl I had seen exactly four years was still disturbing me inside, she was the only cause to my pain and ache I always remain dreaming for her in the day and night, but one day the story changed itself.

Still remember the dawn of that day; I woke prayed to GOD, remembered her and begged almighty to have her glimpse someday and make her mine forever. I went ready for the school, after some classes a seminar was scheduled in the second half; all of us joined there the higher class students were particularly announced to participate and the winner would go to participate in the national speech competition coming in days. The seminar was going on there was pin drop silence in the hall; I buried my face into my hands to get rid of the boring speeches they were giving upfront. My hands start sweating as they usually does when I use to get some discomfort; I heard the anchor screaming the name which I had been obeying into my heart from past three years, precisely he was shouting now '*it's the time to call Saba wani on the stage*" for a speech blessings of sciences the then important essay, hundred percent chances to be asked in the examinations.

The slothfulness seemed going away after hearing her name. Was I dreaming? I put my face into my hands. Was it the mountains of happiness falling over me? I don't know but the thing I could still memorize were the tears my eyes produced after seeing her coming to the dice with some courage and faith.

I still was not prepared to say it a reality, I stood up and wanted to go to meet her on the dice, I squeezed my eyes and patted the backside of my head, and yeah it was Saba from eleventh grade itself, my batch mate but from the section "A". Sections to the students were based on their marks the "A" section contains students over ninety percent; as the sections increased the marks goes decreasing.

The statue I changed in was a dramatic one I continue starring her until her speech was over and believe me I didn't heard anything what she was telling, her gestures were amazing and her lip movement was perfect same like that day. Her speech froze and halted me in every sense. She had become enough skillful and looked a talented lady; it seemed she would never consider me now. Yeah! She was I mean extraordinary.

The chief guest stood up to applaud her finest efforts and she caught lots of young eyeballs especially from the opposite gender.

The seminar was over and everyone rushed out.

Hey sister please stop her I want to talk with her, she is my friend, I shouted at another girl pointing to Saba but she failed to stop Saba, maybe she would have made it but her voice was not enough louder to dominate the noise. She was gone and the other girl too saying sorry. I was very close to my destiny and addressing Saba as my friend was nothing accept a human conduct, humans can do anything for their self satisfaction.

The working day was over we all rushed towards our respective hostels, the night was something full of dreams; I recollected all what I observed and scrutinized throughout the whole day. I felt everything was going into my ways now. It was the first time in decades that I woke up prior every name in the hostel, got ready for the classes, the classes here is again an excuse actually I had grand hunger to see her face and maybe she was going to identify me, I was not sure.

I entered the main door of our noisy class, and the entire class goes nosier when the teacher is on leave. I selected the last bench to keep my hips on, and soon caught an eyeball from a girl fully covered without her eyes. She was not from our section I was sure. Her next step surprised me.

I could see her approaching me.

Hi… she said.

Hi.

You are new, yeah? She said.

Yeah? A new student from the periphery of Kupwara district, keeping my head stooped.

Last day you were squealing, perhaps you wanted to talk with Saba, right?

How did you come to know all this?

I saw you requesting a girl, I was behind you and more over the girl you requested is my friend and the girl you asked for is my best friend.

Oh! That was really a big coincidence and surprise. I was delighted, and I got changed to red of happiness.

Just be normal, I have to ask you something about her.

What do you mean? I start trembling of what she would say next, is she going to tell she had some boyfriend or something horrifying, I waited her to reply.

I mean I would say you something about her going into your favor, she said.

I turned into frank behavior with her after listening those words; I must be I thought she was there to help me or something like that. I started thinking why.

The next question she asked me was something which froze me; she turned candid to ask if I love her.

What should I say I thought before saying anything, I was nervous; I summed up and riposted her in affirmative.

Are you serious? She questioned with her eyebrows up and eyes wide open.

Yeah! More than anyone, I said.

Good to know but you would be wandering how came I know all this, is it?

Obviously I am, not only this I want this story to be discovered to me as soon as you could, I am very eager to know.

Oh! It's as simple as seeing through the air, the case is transparent.

So can you please go ahead? Not taking any advantage like I took in Saba's case years before, she had come to help me out and it doesn't suit to play one more power play.

She started her story if she was narrating it to any author.

"I am her friend; my name is shaziea or you can call me shaazu in short. We met here firstly one year before. There were no usual talks between us, she got her entry directly into the section A of her percentage resulting my removal from the same section because there are only thirty eight students allowed to make up it a complete section, I was the thirty eighth at the time she got her entry which forced me to be in the section B. We became fast friends after, we belong to the same area and I usually use to complain her about my elimination from the top section. She is always frank with me once she discussed her story with me which I suspect was very emotional. She is never that kind of girl people expect her to be. A totally simple one searching for the guy she had seen some five years ago, she knows everything about him, his home, his parents and even his father was her teacher. An ache and distress could be clearly observed on her tiny face, she is very impressed and she wants to talk him but she never found him again. Sam is she told me his name is. Being honest she is actually in love with him perhaps and is impressed deeply by his nature and kindness that blossomed on his face when she met him. You don't

need to be surprised why you were candidly accosted by me. The reason is I just read your name and address on the notice board that exactly matched with what Saba had make me aware of, moreover my doubt changed into reality when I saw you yesterday requesting the girl to call Saba. I request you to please meet her once and just obey whatever she is going to say. She remains silent all the time now her silence can be ceased. She wants you all the time."

Coincidence of the diamond jubilee! Both fell in love at first sight? Shocked me, how could this happen with a guy whose luck had a bad record in the past itself? I wandered; miracles were happening to me that time, it was my luck on its peak leaving the unlucky ghost to the rest. I put my head down before I could say anything, her eyes were focused down to the ground but her ears were attentive that could listen me anyway. I was scared of telling anything not for the reason I had a doubt, but I was not yet sure that my luck had a U turn. The only option to me was now to propose her and start a new life but I decided against it, I want to spend some days with her as a friend so that she could know me well and above all I want her to know that I love her very much before sending her a proposal.

How could I believe she was also suffering from the same quandary? I had a faith in my creator and I believe he will never do the worst or bad with me.

Where is she? I asked her.

She is in the class but she doesn't know you have joined this school, if she would I m sure she would go mad and listen don't ever make it exposed to her until I wouldn't say this best news to her in some delighted and wonderful way.

Okay, I promised I delight.

She went to her class, that day we took 100 percent advantage of the absence of our class teacher, my day started with miracle and let's see what flowers it is going to blossom at its ending.

My day had become worthwhile, happiness and enthusiasm could be seen directly shining on my face.

The day was about to end, due to busy schedule I wasn't to able to go outside till the lectures were over.

I came out of the classes smiling with myself; my mind started framing buildings of dreams for the night, I punched my fist into the air and thanked the creator for what I came across that day.

It was my aim or so called destiny to get her, I had heard that aims can be achieved only after suffering much, seeing much, working much and practicing much, it was perhaps the sole aim which found its destiny without all the words followed by much. Bowing to the creator, dedication, confidence, courage, attitude and faith is something that dominates everything and that were my tools which laid me to my most wanted thing.

Another day was over; I jumped in jubilance, watched outside if I could see one among them either *shaazu* or Saba but no one made it to be them in line of my eyeballs.

Study is the only difficult thing for any student, for me sitting with the text books wide open to gain something of your syllabus is really the hardest time in my life, I never want this, reading my own text books for a minute seems like an hour and I would dream about unnecessary things thousands times plus his eyes would visit the watch hundred times to check the time, it means I totally wasted my time by doing only these two things. This thing was totally opposite when I would found myself in the cricket field where I never get satisfied and would never admit I have played to my full no matter if I had consumed twenty four hours in the playground. What is this I never got and I want to find the root cause behind this. I may say it is the game all about pressure and interest. If you are pressurized you would never get interest, but if there is interest there is no pressure. The text books are something which pays you pressure and to study the big baskets like medical books seems jumping into the fire.

The cause that forced me to touch the interest and pressure is I don't want to get some pressure from any source; I kept the school bag in the corner which wouldn't ever be sighted easily. It was consecutive third day that I wasn't having sympathy for my books.

I was getting my routine a bit changed from worst to not bad; it was my laziness that had gone some other way, I don't know where. Earlier I was late to any work in twenties of minutes but my record is getting better, yesterday I was only ten minutes late in the class, nine minutes late in the mess and some six minutes late to laugh on a joke my friend cracked. Humorous!!!!!

My sentiments never got hurt when some of the guys dubbed me a late factory.

Before I could go to the bed, I made some humorous challenges for myself, first I have to minimize the gap of getting late, the first challenge is to be only five minutes late in the first class and secondly I will open my books for the first time in that week no matter for what time; may be five or ten minutes not exceeding it cause I may get infection. I really couldn't do that, what could my future be, I never know, no aims, hey! I am wrong here I had one aim to get Saba.

I slept without shelving many tensions into my mind but the biggest tension was how and when to get some time to talk with my dream girl.

Chirp…. Chirp…chirp…… chirp ….. Thanks to the birds for the chirping they produced in the mini dawn woke me up. As soon as I opened my eyes her thoughts and the tiny picture came to my mind that resembles how much connected

43

I was getting to her. I brushed my teeth after searching both my toothbrush and paste for ten minutes they were placed at the right place; I got them beneath my pillow.

I bathed for at least twenty minutes, removed all the wax from my big ears, I had some bleeding through my nose because the hard booger I tried to pull out had a strong hug with the walls of my nostrils, but failed to pull it out and opted to left that job to be accomplished at last. Till then it would smoothen.

I came back from the bathroom, got ready for the classes. The absence of mirror in my room was creating problems. I wore all the uniform in hurry, the socks I wore I wore it inside out and rushed out quickly.

I went to see my face in to the bikes' mirror standing some steps away from the main hostel gate, oh shit, what the fuck I was doing in the bathroom for twenty plus minutes, it would have been better to look after the cattle for those twenty minutes. Nothing was wrong but a big booger ball was hanging from my left nostril. I saw left and then right making sure no one could see me what I could do next, it become hard to do what I was going to do when you had no handkerchief but it was a simple one for me, I picked the cloth from the seat and cleaned my nose, kept it clandestinely at its own place.

I visited the mirror again but don't found any hurdle on my face, I was perfect to enter the school, I thanked the bike owner.

I was some steps away from my class room when my ears made the lecture perceivable with my chest some inches wider than yesterday. I set my eyes through the opened door; saw the teacher writing something as I noticed a vacant place on the desk on the left hand side of the door. The extreme wide teacher with his stomach talking to his thighs wasn't enough witty to move swiftly so I think taking of a chance. As I saw him turning to the black board I rushed in undisclosed and opted to sit on the front bench.

Hey! This man is wiser, the words I could hear when he focused his big red eyes onto mine.

Yes sir! I was terrified. I thought he had seen me coming in.

Good boy and hats off you, he was thrilled and showed his big white teeth.

I was flummoxed searching for what I did which he liked.

I don't say anything nor does him and went to teach the physics problem.

It was the first time I was getting what was being taught, it was very difficult to hear the teacher and his writings had a unique style, it was tough to get it from that corner, but few students did.

He finished and asked the students to ask some questions if any regarding the topic.

There were no questions. Everyone looked eyes into eyes and everyone start moving their eyebrows to one another.

It was a simple problem, sir everyone would have got it, I said.

I think you get it Sam?

I mixed up to say yes, I was afraid. But I summed up and replied in an affirmative.

Students it is the hardest problem in you physics book I think either everyone or no one has got it. That is why you avoid asking questions. Is it?

If anyone who got it can raise hands. He said.

I was enough fast to raise my hand for the true reason. I got the problem clearly. Mine was the only one hand soaring which took the oxygen out of me. I was happy and felt confidence over myself for the first time.

Only one, the teacher said smiling, I could get that was a sad smile.

Ok good, it fantastic I will repeat it, before that Sam will make you understand the problem.

I got up, solved and presented it to the students.

Give a big hand to him; everybody did and made me feel lf I was in a chapatti factory.

What the teacher went on to teach next was amazing.

Today Sam has made me to touch this, today I will say you how success kisses your feet.

See this boy has proved his thirst of getting things; he shifted from the last bench to the front one. I liked it. He said.

Thanks to the rest of people in the class who managed to keep their teeth unseen besides knowing what the reality was.

It was the first time some teacher had boosted me up that too for a false reason. Had he known the reality, I would have been out of the class for a week, he was enough strict in terms of discipline. Inefficiency was not a big concern for him because he was a knack trainer who used to train students in a loving way, but he never compromised with indiscipline. Alas! He wasn't the quickest to get what I did.

He went next.

You are a new student, yeah? Pointing to me, he said.

Yes sir. I replied.

Ok good you look creative enough. He admitted.

There was no answer for this, I managed to say, can't say sir, if you think I am I must be then.

He liked my answer and declared it a creation of a healthy mind and patted me and run his hand through my hair tenderly.

Please have some attention. Today you will get some lesson practically, he warned to listen it carefully.

He went like this.

*Sam the only student who got the problem, the toughest one. Students never make it to understand in the first attempt. Sam got it only after bringing some changes into him. When I asked if you had got it, nobody had questions in their minds nor did anybody ask me to repeat in order they could get it properly. It is your right to ask a teacher to repeat it no matter how many times. Not getting it is not your fault but not asking me to repeat is your biggest fault. There is no shortcut to success, for this you must have to bring in you what you don't possess or the tools of greatness we can say. Greatness always comes before and after success; you can't say a person is great but not successful. You can say he is successful but not great. "To achieve greatness you must need to be successful and to be successful you need to be great". Something is lacking in you that is why you don't get it, let me explain. This desk on the front was vacant for several minutes and now you can see Sam sitting on it, a boy who had already got parked himself in the corner on a well designed desk. Who persuades him or who motivates him to select the front one, and why? Can anybody among you answer me please? It's ok don't be puzzled I will take you to that point. It was nothing else but his satisfaction and hunger backed by willingness and attitude that crafted to modify him. It is what builds a man urges him and flies him to his milestone. **Satisfaction,** take it to you greatest level, a man never get satisfied but you can take it to the point wherefrom you could realize something was good. Sam doesn't get satisfied in the last bench so he migrated only to see the board properly that satisfies him. **Hunger,** Feel some hunger inside you to get things in the proper way. Sam had a hunger to grasp and understand the problem which boldly prepared him to go to the front. "If you had hunger to get things properly the distance to your destiny gets halved". **Willingness,** never let this point down ever, it seems simple but has a great impact. If you are eager and ready to do then never look forward. Never took it same as hunger. If Sam wasn't getting satisfied and he has hunger* *to learn the problem but he was not willing to leave the bench to come up front he wouldn't had got the problem in the best ways.* **Attitude,** *Think out of the box, think I am the best and work accordingly. Think in a specific way and be creative enough search for the new innovative ways and never lose any opportunity in your life that could make you great. Sam thought differently than rest of you, got an opportunity, used it and got what was a toughest of problems. So I think you go it to your best.*

All he did boosted us up to be straight forward, frank, handworker and dedicated. He persuades us to be great one day. I did a mini thing that took a false intention made us to get the greatest of topics. I was extremely impressed by the motivation skill, art, experience and knowledge of the teacher who builds a meaningful class out of what was simply an untrue change. The skill of inducing all the success tools and relating it with the simple change was simply amazing, I liked it.

The topic deposited something in my mind and in no to go time that teacher became illustrious to me. He changed my fate and destiny with that speech; I got boosted up to do something magnificent.

I was an ordinary boy with some ordinary thoughts and till that date I was never known to my destiny. I was very careless about my future and predictions were made I can do nothing in my life all around. The lecture clearly outlines that; *"He who has hunger to be great never gets satisfied and is always willing to do anything to get that satisfaction leading him to get enough attitudes which brings his success".*

The speech got me changed; I got it clearly from up to down. Even I also know I wasn't the talented guy at all. The biggest problem was not that physics teacher got me as a talented student, my image is high, and I am an extraordinary student in his views but how to continue this impression was definitely a problem. It becomes hard for an average student to continue such impressions. I was not an excuse. I need to study very hard for one more big reason that was to get Saba it was my challenge. She is the topper of the class and I am at the last how could she consider me. It doesn't suit.

The result of the seminar was announced, some students were selected to produce speeches at the inter school level. I don't know the names but one of our classmates produced sounds like that. He also added the selected students are five in strength two from our batch and they are leaving by tomorrow. The competition was getting tough.

The class was over and we had a free class to follow, I opted to seek them out and I left for the same leaving my bag in the class itself.

I rummaged around but don't found them.

My head went down in despondence to step towards my own class, I was sweating, and the thirty five minutes investigation was in vain.

I entered into my class and found my bag opened and books exposed. I was worried that I had been pilfered by any larcener. But those books had a greater value. I explored my bag and found everything safe and full. I zipped my bag wrote a half day leave and went off. The day furnishes some happiness at its beginning and tensions thereafter. I don't have her glimpses yet again and how to handle physics sir was the colossal apprehension.

Unlike yesterday I made myself prepared to solve another physics problem in the evening it was actually my first attempt to do so in these years. I opened the mighty book and soon got flabbergasted.

As soon I opened the book some piece of paper full of writing was exposed.

I found a paragraph written over it. I had no interest to read it charged up and start shredding it before my eyes fell onto a word which ceased me. I was surprised, the word was *Saba*.

I became eager to read it. Reading these words was if the sun start rising from the west for me.

#Sam

Hey Sam, where are you? I am shaazu. Saba is unaware about this letter it is from me only. We came here to search you, and I told everything to Saba except you love her cause it is something which you had to say in best possible ways. She doesn't believe it, but I proved it to her anyway. She is crazy to see you. Don't bother about anything; Saba is one among the selectees in the speech competition and she needs your praise to win the competition. Initially after listening about you she preferred to see you rather to go there but I insisted her to go which she agreed later at. She had a sturdy crave to get her eyes into yours but your absence in the class made her poignant. You don't feel any despondency regarding her; You will not be able to see both of us for next week or so.. We went on to write you in order you could get the cause of not finding us too. Have a nice day stay blessed, Saba will be able to talk to you only after coming back but if you are here then please meet us before we could leave. We will be waiting in front of administration block exact ten minutes before our departure which is at 4pm. Do come if you want. Bye, stay blessed and take you absolute care. We are always with you.

Shaazu

Oh! What a mess it happened. Oh my God why don't I read it in the class; was all I managed to shout. I deposited my head into my palms.

My mood changed, I start thinking about it. It bestowed me enough sadness and I found it very difficult to read that day. I closed my book and preferred to go to the bed.

The day was gone; it was easy to meet them provided if I could have seen the letter in the day time before 4pm. That is so called time and tide waits for none. My time was gone. I start thinking what could have happened if I could have seen the letter. I went to the bed taking these thoughts away.

3:50 pm completes ten minutes waiting them but they are still unseen. Her narrated time is approaching it is exact three fifty by my watch.

Oh! It starts drizzling. The wind also starts blowing faster leading the rain to fall in the V shape.

The drizzle got heavier now; it might force me to leave that place.

I made my mind not to leave because I wanted my eyes to go with something that could disturb me during nights.

I looked up and saw a couple of girls coming towards me with something in their hands.

One of them gestured me in some romantic way. I don't know what it was, kissing the hand and blowing it to me. It contains kiss so I called it a romantic gesture. I had no answer but smiled.

As they came closer I got them.

Two girls of the same height but their body structure differs, I got it was my fishy lady and shaazu. Saba walked keeping her head down and the other had her up.

Shaazu said something to me pointing towards her, I don't hear because of the distance but they smiled and I too joined them. Raindrops start dropping from my hairs and nose. I got totally wet now.

I was confused what to do; firstly I thought to spread my arms to welcome Saba and then stand still with my eyes focused on the ground because it seemed odd to spread my arms as she was not my girlfriend or wife.

I found them in front of me. I shake hands with *Shaazu* she greeted me and I followed her. I looked into Saba's eyes and turned into a statue, I was dumbfounded. I became unable to speak for a minute, all I did was focused my eyes into hers until she was effected with emotions. I could see her eyes producing tears. I am stupid, I am sorry, with this I got my handkerchief and start wiping her eyes.

Yeah you are most stupid I hate you. She said emotionally.

She looked enough pretty telling me stupid, her voice wasn't getting to its maximum. My eyes got affected as well.

I hugged her firmly she was very smooth and the rain was just amazing.

Shaazu herself got taste of some tears; she smiled while cleaning her eyes too. They were the tears of happiness.

The hug was a special one I found myself into heavens; I got immense coolness inside, my heart start murmuring once more. I feel the world is mine but it was early to think beyond that because we were yet to say we love one another.

The romance in rain had always become a mighty prey to great poets and in films the combination had earned its special spot but today I was practicing it in reality.

She handed over the gift to me, I accepted but I had nothing to give her back.

I went to see her once again but I had no courage to stop my eyes to get glimpses of her beautiful face. She was a changed girl and enough developed in every possible ways.

Her hair was long beyond my notion. Her eyebrows were thin like a black thread, her lips were fleshy and pinky enough. Her chest has acquired a good height, and her long legs add it the most. Her waist was developed more rounded, and the accent too was changed into a soft musical tone she was composing her talks quiet beautifully. I am the man who can measure her development accurately because all the things I discussed I know them since years. I still remember the day when I utilized accurately and effectively that power play. I know one can realize development when he catches glimpses of the same things after a definite time gap and so was the case with me.

We talked less but wiped our eyes more. Suddenly she said she is going to the completion and she wants my praise and added she will be back after a week, if no then it will turn into a nine day journey.

You trust my praise? I questioned her.

What a stupid question it is, I trust you more than me. She said.

It was not something to be surprised upon I know we too loved one another yet to verbalize.

She was leaving the bus was ready to depart, she said me good bye both verbally and non-verbally so did I.

The gift was very heavy; I rushed my hostel, I was eager to open it. I sat on the bed, and opened it from the polythene; it was glittering inside.

You don't know what my reaction was when *shaazu* told me about you, welcome back; let's start our life with new gears halting old tears. It was all I could read, written over the first covering.

I removed the opening shining covering with a flash of smile.

There were three more, I removed them all.

Now I was only one slit afar to get the glance of the gift.

Peep.….peep.….Peep.….peep.……peep.……peep.…… peep.…peep.…peep.….peep.……   peep.….peep.…….. peep.…….. What is it? The clock was alarming it was 5:00 am.

I opened my mind searched for the gift like a nutty man. I screamed for my gift but find nothing looked down in emotions and didn't move for some minutes.

It was a dream that only tasted me the fake reality; I want to fuck dreams which make us to cry. I start talking to myself, picked that letter hugged it and went to sleep again. That letter calmed me down; proved everything was fine at least I came to know Saba is here and she is coming back soon.

Suddenly I got myself able-bodied. I decided to bunk for that day and it proved a reality. The other days went good in the classes. Several days passed and one day *shaazu* was seen without Saba under a tree reciting some verses.

I step towards her, as usual greeted her and so did her and I questioned about Saba.

What she replied was pleased as well as astounding.

Congrats!! Her journey turned in to nine days as she got selected for the finals. She looks good to win the competition; she is working hard only to make you feel proud. She said with her noise on a good height.

Oh! That is really a good new, my praise is always with both of you, but tell me does she ever talk me if she would win that competition asked a stupid question.

You stupid! You are very special for her she can't ever forget you, I know. She hit me on my right cheek.

Ok, tell me good news about Saba. I requested her.

Saba is very nice and intelligent and mature. She is going to win the finals and hopefully she will get here in three days. She told if she was telling it to a kid.

I got everything in that sentence; I mumbled the word mature again and again attempting to get it described briefly. Actually I was happy to listen that word, no matter to what thing she has compared it, it will be enough good if she had compared it with her structure, I was sure it is not be so but I still went to ask to get it clearly.

Hey! Why you look bewildered, is there anything wrong in the word is used for her? If so I am sorry then.

No it is up to the mark, I liked it that is why I am puzzled. But can you please elaborate the word *"mature"* briefly I had a doubt regarding its comparison.

Don't try to be over smart, my dear Sam, she spanked my shoulder. I liked it the most. And we both laughed.

Get me to that point, please.

I mean she know what is good and what is bad, is very serious to her studies, talks less but momentous.

That sentence made me some bit sad initially as it was not compared with her structural development; made me happy in the middle but changed me to feel anxiety at last. It is not good if she talks less, how we could be romantic after getting into love, at least she should talk me for hours to bring some romantic flow, electrification and enthusiasm. I like romance and it adds when you would get something amorous to hear from the one you love.

Does she really talk less? I asked her helplessly.

Yes, is there anything wrong?

It is okay but how does you manage to be her best friend if she talks less, I mean do you ever get bored.

What a babyish question. She is very frank with me; she talks with her friends and amuses them very much but not with others.

I got it, I was jubilated. If she amuses friends then why can't me…. but I would laugh over the ardent jokes. I thought it all inside.

I am going now, we had a class. She asked me.

Ok you can, and thanks.

Thanks for what?

Because I had no words to tell you after you became best friends with me. I said with some simplicity into my head.

Oh! Don't try to be so formal, avoid this word to be used to friends. Thanks and friends always run parallel.

I revered her for telling me that much about Saba moreover she helps me neglect the word thanks.

Bye she said.

Ok bye……..meet you soon. I said hopefully.

I caught the path of my hostel to step over for at least ten minutes till I reached there. Had everything and start doing what I had been trying my best since days but was yet to do, it was reading. I preferred physics but I was heartily connected with English.

Nothing went into my mind to be praised in physics class tomorrow, I switched to another book and it was all bouncers I was getting from the mathematics, I closed it in dismay rubbed my mind for two minutes, found nothing except pain.

I had no options to do for that day after the study failure.

I exercised for some minutes but nothing was getting in my favor. I start imagining about the almonds the only thing which could make my mind sharp to get these problems. Kashmir is full of almond trees, and it is believed they can build your mind strong but it was yet to get into practice. I need to do something I know. I need to be in the section 'A' next year, if I want to earn her which needs hard work, headword and hand work. I put a challenge to work up with the three works to get my mission completed. More over I was yet to set my target while all others had theirs, some wanted to become doctors some engineers some civil servants some writers but I was the one with no aim. When asked about my aim in the very first class, I bowed my head and start thinking what to say, others went laughing and perhaps I had forgot I had taken admission in the most popular school where students are very extraordinary no matter they belong to sections based on the grading systems, there was only micro difference in the percentage if someone is a single percent ahead of you this means there is a minimum gap of fifty students between you two. Being inferior to your wife isn't good I could understand it and its dire consequences are not worth to be forgotten. A husband must be virtuous so that a wife should feel safe and proud. It also don't suit that your wife is doing the maximum I believe.

Four days passed as they were passing, no study, and no home work. It was Saba all over roaming into my head.

There was no source to get some information about Saba; even pigeons have become expensive and inefficient now.

I went to school as usual on the fifth day. We had two classes already. *Shaazu* came to me running hold my hand and showed me the notice board. There were several news on that, I am trying my best to find such news which made *Shaazu* to bring me here, all seemed not of that type, *Shaazu* had her eyes in mine but I was totally concentrated towards the notice board.

I questioned what was special which made you so crazy.

See with my eyes, you will get. She cracked the typical Kashmiri proverb and smiled. Picked my forefinger and kept it on the headline. All I could see was very pleasant and cheery. The news was about Saba. It was written......... *"Sky touch girl wins the onerous speech competition"*. My joy knew no bounds after reading this. I smiled and smiled in jubilance for the success of such a girl who loves me. I was sure there is a strong support from her side as well, finding myself deep into her love.

Where is she? I asked *Shaazu* about *Saba*.

She is in her class. She said.

I could see teachers entering the section "A" but I don't know what they do there, I think they must be congratulating Saba.

I want to meet her, I requested *Shaazu*.

Let the teacher and student horde go down, I will pull her out to meet you. She said.

Ok, I will be waiting till then I am going to my class, I said and she replied accordingly obeying my sayings.

Our physics sir was teaching in the class unfortunately he had a chair under his hips pointed towards the class. I glanced from the ajar he was exposed demanding for a physics book. He starts reading it with immense interest placing it parallel to his eyes making a 90 degree angle. He fenced all what he could see in front of him, I thought I can change this into my fortune as the attendance was something not to let pass.

I opened the door slightly making sure not to let it to jangle.

It turned into my luck as he remained still till I choose the front bench to sit on. All the classmates flashed into a chortle.

No jokes please. He warned the class.

Listening to the retort all the students got me to burst into a bulky guffaw, as they know the teacher had got it wrong once again.

He offended and screamed…….. Hey! I want no jokes in the class, understand!!!!!!!

That deafening sound soon bunged all the mouths in that class except his. I put down my head and he went on.

Sam?

Yes sir.

Get up and write the names of those who are making any kind of sounds.

This sentence now becomes my source to laugh. I declared the sentence as an act of injustice; I thought and laughed loudly.

Sam? Why are you laughing? The teacher screamed.

Nothing sir! I thought inside that mouth only was not the organ to produce sounds there were some other, I was puzzled how to behave if someone does it. I think you got why I laughed.

Anyway he doesn't mind I was laughing and went on to his job, the 90 degree reading.

Soon the bell rang for lunch break when the board had no name written over it.

I could see *Shaazu* from the opened door I came to know who may be with her.

The teacher prepared himself to leave after ordering me to sit down and added. Any roll numbers?

No sir.

He tapped my shoulder before giving a dirty look and went out.

I rushed outside and saw nothing.

I start roaming outside the room making sure I could be seen by them. My both hands were deposited into the deep pockets.

I could see pair of girls approaching me as I rushed into the classroom after identifying *Shaazu*. I knew who the second one was. It was hard to guess her as we hadn't seen each other since years. Even harder to believe that such beautiful face was going to be mine for generations to come. They came closer and I hid into the class. I was confused what to do in front of such a beautiful face, have I the ability to do everything right? I am from a village and she too is but is way ahead of me, a winner of a tough speech competition, an extraordinary student, beautiful, most respected student and frank these were all the things which pressurized me. I was very sacred to talk such a lady who is superior to me in every department.

I kicked these thought out, and thought to meet her frankly congratulating her to win the competition.

I became red, *Shaazu* was gesturing me to come out to meet Saba, a girl who had become a frequent visitor to my soul, a girl whose sketch was with me for years to talk with, a girl who admire me the most, a girl a cause to my eyes to change into waterfalls, a girl who is predicted to be all mine, a girl whose structure always disturbed my mental innocence, a girl who make me cry and a girl for whom I want to die.

I walked outside with a low footfall.

I remained thunderstruck; my eyes got flabbergasted over the shape they got to see. I was going mad of happiness. I couldn't believe was it a reality or not, I wasn't yet prepared to declared it a reality rather it was a dream come true. The girl who used to come into my dreams was only inches afar me, a girl who use to come to my mind as an imagination was a reality in front of me. What to do next I don't know, my eyes remained into hers for longer time, I want to hug and kiss her rosy lips but the surrounding was not clear, hell to it. I remained looking into her clear black eyes and all I could see was my face from her eyeballs, all happened like it happened in the dream but the rain was lacking. My eyes became too sensitive to emotions, I snivel and soon burst into tears, she followed me and made her face look much brighter with the tears. I want to drink the teardrop hanging from her right cheek, I couldn't see rain drops hanging from her face but I was surprised they were all tears, she look prettier than before, her development talks.

I don't want my eyes to get off from her beautiful face.

We had a hand shake after five minutes approximately, her hand was as smooth as her heart, I glanced it was very shiny and clear. I felt some coolness inside; I felt my life as smooth as her lips appeared to be. It looked if she dropped tones of happiness into my heart and soul after the hand shake.

How are you my life? Oh it's not life it's ah…ah…pipe, no…no…no…knife, no…wipe, no…no…no…no… wife, no…no…no…no… I am sorry. I got mixed up and there was no word which could be rhymed with life to prove it was a mistake.

Why are you very serious, it happens, it's not a crime. She was sobbing.

There was simplicity, clarity and honesty in that beautifully composed voice, I wish I could hug the voice she produced.

She was getting very emotional, perhaps she loves me more that I love her, I thought. She was looking very serious she was lacking control over her voice.

Why are you so serious, why are you doing it, I will be available to you twenty four into seven. I said.

Don't lie, you stupid she sobbed again.

Yes I am stupid the biggest stupid and careless person, please stop it now *Ghaashu [the light of my eyes]*. I am always with you.

She flashed into a big laugh after hearing the word *Ghaashu [the light of my eyes]*. Was it again a mistake from my side? No, never I deliberately said that.

It was after several years that my eyes have got her glimpse, she was totally changed and enough developed.

I too became unable to control, I laughed too.

You have developed over the years, I said after finding nothing to say.

Everyone does I am not an exception, she replied.

I don't care about everything when such beautiful treasure is going to become mine forever. I said.

What do you mean?

I mean you.

She laughed and I accompanied her.

Her laughter touched my heart and I desire she could laugh again but for that I want to do something funny. I wished I could ask her each and every teardrop that how beautiful her eyes were from inside. But it was not difficult but impossible. I wondered how beautiful she would be internally. I could see there were several waterways of tears on her cheeks, they had made shiny roads some run down her cheeks and some other way, I peeked one leading to her lips. I wished to be a tear drop so that I could reach to her lips to kiss them after that I wished to enter into her mouth and get swallowed so that I could witness how beautiful she looks inside, and how managed her organs are. She was really wonderful; kindness was simply blossoming on her beautiful face.

I got myself a prey of romantic imaginations.

What a big fuss she has, a lovely face with smooth and healthy fat cheeks slightly rosy beneath the eyes, I looked into her eyes for several minutes while biting by lips. We came closer and soon our gap was reduced to naught. We hugged each other very tightly; her chest was a difference, I run my right hand behind her head and my left one down her right forearm to bring her more closer, her fleshy chest was enough smooth to put me in excitement it looked if my chest had two big balloons beneath it. I helped her hair behind her ears from both sides, and then accumulated her cheeks with my forefinger and thumb. I was taking maximum advantage of such time; we both brought one more eye contact. She was red and me too, we both start biting our lips again and I start diminishing our lip gap, as soon as our lips come enough closer we opened our mouths to get each other's lips inside. I was electrified inside when I got her lower lip into my mouth and she got my upper, we kissed each other very smoothly and soon I was wild, we shared kilos of saliva. Our teeth don't disturb us, I took her tongue and sucked it wildly, she start producing sexy sounds, she wanted more and more from a guy who was at his peak. I pulled my hand back and start rubbing her chest with a great enthusiasm after finding something even fleshier; she was going crazy her hair went totally confused. I would never say that the trousers start some moment beneath my belly. I was feeling some pain from there but the excitement dominates it. My hands were doing a terrific job both from her behind and front. I sucked her neck and ears and soon started sucking her chocolaty chest and hugged her strongly.

Hey! Sam what are you thinking, was all I could hear. This astounded me and put my imagination hanging.

Nothing, I said incredulity.

In no to go time after realizing what it was I checked my zip innocently after hanging my head and behaved if I examined my feet, fortunately there was no destruction, my zip was okay and no liquid was seen.

What if I could have done all what I imagined?

I know I couldn't do it at such places. She gave her hand and we had a hand shake, she uttered, friends forever.

I too did the same plus *Shaazu*.

She told that she will definitely meet me in the evening, I was happy. I wanted to talk her for much time but there was a scarcity of time and site. I looked her from behind she was very fleshy and it adds when you could guess the body size, thanks to the tailor who had sieved her body fitted uniform.

I desperately waited for the evening we were both in hostels. There is always a strict rule for girls in the hostel especially when it is co-educated institution; girls are not allowed to go outside after 6pm while boys hadn't any rule, if there is some rule like this then it is not wrong to say you could always see a big giant puncture into the fencing or there must be lots of bricks and stones accumulated under the base of the fence making it easier to climb and jump outside. Even girls also fuck this strictness' but couldn't do what boys do.

There was a canteen in the campus where boys and girls use to visit to have something to drink or eat. I waited there for some minutes before they approached, I knew it was again a fucking time as it was approaching to 6pm I preferred to quit from there because ten minutes were not enough to talk. It was the favorite evenings of the week not for me but for whole students across the globe, can you guess absolutely you can it was Saturday evening.

We can talk whole day tomorrow I think and went to my room. It was good to avoid them because I will not be satisfied with ten minutes and these ten minutes will surely become a cause to miss her in the night. I left that place.

The birds had always a non rhythm chirping music in the mornings but it was still the music people love the most, I love to hear it. This day the chirruping was simply unstoppable, perhaps the birds were enjoying the Sunday dawn, I looked through the window it was drizzling, the atmosphere was pleasant and the ground was wet. Clouds could be seen in the sky making the dawn darker than rest of the days. It looked if it was December morning in Kashmir. I got maybe the birds got unsheltered and that maybe the cause of their crying or may be the birds want to sleep more; or maybe they were cursing the rain, my mind manufactured these thoughts for them. Unlike students birds and animals don't have holidays to think to gossip all around. Rainy mornings and nights give a wonderful sleep; everyone loves to hear the clatter the rain use to make after striking the metallic roof. I had roommates who would warn you not to make any type of sound or noise till 11:00 am on Sundays'. They even don't bother about the breakfast.

I obeyed the rule as others, got myself out of the quilt, the clock shows it was 9:30 still very careful, I don't want to disturb others not for the reason they may get irritated but I was sure they would kill me if I do that.

I bathed, perfumed and oiled. I looked enough smart at the time when rest of my roommates were still snoring.

I Went to the canteen to have something and had chapattis and potatoes with a cup of tea; the best dish I could taste in mornings.

Girls must have some same rules like boys to follow in the hostels; no girl was seen till the watch showed eleven.

I went back to my hostels got myself changed from trousers to pant shirt. The jean pant possesses new fashion, the bottom tight.

I waited impatiently for them, I roamed here and there, and I was restless. My parents were also not coming that day as they had a visit recently. I could hear the noises of the warden; he was screaming the names of those whose parents had come. Students would enter and exit all the footsteps and the vocal noise would make an echo not good for ears.

After some minutes my ears got something to hear, *"Sam, come out your parents had come"*.

It was an innocent immature male sound. The sound struck and I was out, I couldn't find my parents I questioned the little boy who brought this news and he innocently replied, "Your parents hadn't come but your girlfriend taught me to call you out with that sentence only".

I smiled. And he looked into my face with innocence. How did a boy of nine or ten got she was my girlfriend, I wondered.

Ok, tell me how you got she is my girlfriend, I questioned him.

Simple brother, she is big, you are big, she is beautiful, you are smart, she has craze, you have craze, she want to see you, you rushed out quickly, its love and nothing else, he responded and I tapped his hand and went to laugh.

hahaha ok tell me where they are? I questioned him.

In the ground, he replied.

Come with me, I will complain that you call her as my girlfriend. And do you know she will kill you. I said with a mood.

He cried, and managed to say, no…no…no…no…please let me go.

I let him go and smiled proving I was joking.

I will complain to the principal, you had a girlfriend, he said after giving me a polluted look.

I smiled again.

I am also joking have fun, bye, he said and I followed him.

I could see the ground from a distance of 200 meters, I could see everyone without identification the ground was colored, different people had different dresses.

I walked continuously, the boy made a mistake by not being straight forward; I could have perfumed myself again.

I start stepping bigger and bigger and soon reached them. As usual the greetings were something I uttered first up.

Saba was dressed green from top to bottom, even her slippers were green. She had a great impression of being matching.

How are you, she said.

I am fine, I answered.

You look very nice; she appreciated the new bottom tight jeans.

I know green women, I asked.

I know, she said, she took revenge.

She had a brown colored hair that looked extreme red against the sunlight, I was enough creative to compare her with a maize. Yes she looked 100 percent like maize, with her hair tied and hanged from behind.

4

The journey starts as Friends

She requested and I sat down. *Shaazu* was at her own heights, she too looked quiet pretty, but Saba was a great example of nature's beauty. She started her conversation touching my family background.

You are from *Drugmulla,* am I right?

Yeah, I know my cousin sister must have told you, isn't it?

Absolutely, but note she hadn't told me everything ok? She said.

Don't panic I will make you aware about each and every thing, I said.

Ok, what is your father? She questioned first up.

My father is a teacher in government middle school located at a walking distance from our home. His name is *Ghulam Ahmad Shah* and murmured "Enough strict" keeping this as secret as I don't want his character to make me a prey to trifling questions. Girls usually do that and its very tough to answer them. My mom *Mehfooza* is a domestic manager. I kept my information going.

It sounds good; she repeated my mother's name.

How many are you.

We are six, me, the eldest, my brother *Aaqib* and 4s's.

Eldest and 4s's she repeated it, what is 4s's.

These are the names of my four sisters, every name starts with the letter "S".

How sweet, names please, she said smiling.

Sakeena, my younger, *Sahiba, Aaqib's* younger, twins *Suhana* and *Shaista* the youngest. All are students.

It is your turn now. I said.

My father is a tailor; his name is *Muhammad Raheem Wani* and *Hajira wani* respectively. We are four, my eldest brother *Sajjad,* working in J&K Police, *Suhail, sajjad's* younger also working in the same department. My sister *Ruqiya* a final year student younger than, *Suhail.* And I am the youngest.

I got they had a combination of 3s's too. *Saba, Suhail, Sajjad.*

You are the youngest, I said.

Yeah, but it's too tough to be the youngest, the eldest ones possesses the supreme power, always use to put you in hard works, I did the maximum at home since my eight class. And everyone would scold me even on diminutive things. She replied.

No, it's not the case with everyone; at least I don't practice this. We are from Indian villages where people are very conservative. Every guardian keeps putting some pressure on a girl child here. About boys no one bothers. Our culture, our values and our civilization differ from western, where everything is fare anywhere. I said.

Yeah, we are the best people in the world. She said.

Everyone is best, but keep looking up the environment you are having. Do things which are digestible and acceptable.

You can do all in India what you can enjoy openly in European countries. The thinking and the perception of the people differs. We need to be accordingly. I said.

I need an example for what we can't do which European can enjoy openly. She said.

Just leave it, you can't understand.

Please, make me clear, she said.

She was totally innocent; she hadn't any idea what I was saying.

What you are thinking about, she said.

See, have you seen people here kissing one another at public places? I questioned her.

Oh! Shit what you are saying. Is that an example? Not, at all never but it is the easiest way to make you understand. I said.

But European people can do it easily on public places, Indians use to greet and shake hands when they meet someone for the first time in the day while European don't practice this all; they use to kiss each other's lips when so. If you would visit some place there you will find people practicing this as common as plants in the nursery.

Ha ha ha ha ha ha ha ha, she flashed into a giant laugh. You are so funny; you gave humorous but accurate examples.

I too smiled, her smile makes me to laugh, and she was pretty, the more of her prettiness was getting exposed the more I was getting euphoric.

You looked very innocent the day you were telling lots of things with your head down. I mean in your JNV several years before. She said.

Yeah I know, six years before.

Yeah you are right, it's absolutely six years. She said after doing some calculation on her fingers.

I never said her it was you with your head bowed all time and you don't know what advantage I took from it, I thought inside.

One thing one thing let you mention your proper address. I requested her.

Bumhama, she said.

It was a walking distance from our home, but we don't know one another even it was the case with me and rest of our villagers as well, because I was a kid when I joined boarding school.

How you joined this school. She said.

My percentage in JNV model school was continuously diminishing. That is why, I said.

Any reason for that, she said.

Here was a chance to propose her by saying the cause were you, but I thought it is not the smartest ways to tell the beautiful combination of words for which I was waiting years.

Not any big reasons, I was totally diverted to English, I want to become a writer and I will prove it one day. I said.

That is great, I am dull in English, hope you would teach me the grammar, she said.

Ok, I will, you will get trained in months. I said smiling.

Hope so. She said.

But what is your aim, I said.

I want to become a doctor, I am very good in science, she said

That is very good, it means you would teach me the rest of subjects, I said

Oh! Hoo I am not that much brilliant but I will try. She said and looked a bit shocked. But I think I would never learn English, she added.

This is your problem, I said

How you can say like that, she said.

No one is genius in any department but they are interested into it, keeps them super linked and consuming time on that which automatically makes them the master, I said.

That is good, interest and time is very important, she said.

Yeah, *"To think only others are brilliant is not brilliance but crushing your own brilliancy, brilliance is to find and adopt their brilliancy to make you brilliant"* I said.

It is awesome, she said in a jiffy.

It's unfair to think they are brilliant not for others but for yourself, everyone is brilliant and can do anything by working hard over it, to admit others brilliant is nothing other than a source of pressure which automatically brings your hopes and brilliancy down.

That is really great. I appreciate you, I am happy to be with such a person who has depth of knowledge and talent. It will be a wonderful journey ahead. She said.

I am sorry but you deserve thanks for that. I said.

She acknowledges me once more by admitting my words supreme.

I have to ask you one more important thing, can I? She said.

Absolutely, why not, I said quickly.

You love anyone, I mean someone you have crush on she put her head down.

Hahahahaha Not at all, neither a crush nor love but I can say she is everything to me but I can't tell you the name. I said.

Please, please, I want to hear her name, she requested.

No I can't. I can tell you the starting and ending letter of her name only. I said.

Ok. She said.

Her name starts with "S" and ends with "A".

No, you need to tell the full name as majority of the female names in Kashmir starts with S and ends with A. I can give you thousand names that don't mean everyone has your crush upon. She said.

Absolutely not, but she is very special for me, I love her very much. I said.

Even I too know that there were already two names possessing these traits in front of me. That was the reason to tell her such name.

Her face was getting pale, but she doesn't comment over it more.

Do you love someone? My soul doesn't allow me but I asked.

Yeah I too love someone, she said with quiet gloominess.

Name, I said.

No need to tell you, I will tell you once we will be good friends till then I am sorry. I can't.

It looked serious from her side, but the story *Shaazu* had told me earlier is unforgettable. I knew she was taking revenge.

I ordered some meal from the nearby restaurant and start having it, it was fried chicken with chapattis; no one is allowed to go outside of hostels so we start eating it in the ground itself.

I am the biggest meat eater in my family, we finished it very soon, *Shaazu* looked to have the same traits but Saba was depressed, she had only one that too took long time to get swallowed. I knew what the problem was with her. It gives me a poof it was a double sided love. *Shaazu* is pointing towards Saba to show me something which I don't get. Saba looked very depressed, she was all right before I announced my love life.

There was no point of romance which I had thought to give a glimpse of, not talking about the kisses or more than that but my throat was there to utter rather to practice.

I knew *Shaazu* since some months by Saba but we both where enough frank with each other. She knows we love one another but was yet to propose Saba, I love Saba even I know she loves me too and Saba loves me she knows this but does I love her was still she could know. It was a double sided love for me only but a single sided for her. Situations were getting very emotional. I gave a clue of my love life which made her depressed clearly visible.

The conversation between us was over as the bell rang divulgating girls and junior boys for lunch. The rules in our school were enough strict, girls and juniors were treated carefully.

Saba and *Shaazu* were about to leave, *Shaazu* waved her hand to say good bye but Saba don't said anything, she looked talking to herself and went away.

I am sorry not to obey Gandhijis' lessons he gave through one of his monkeys of not seeing bad, I thought to utilize that time effectively so I started seeing her from behind. It is a universal fact 99 percent of males would see females mostly from backside. I wonder why ladies go on wasting their time in decorating their faces if they are going to be visualized mostly from their posterior part, just consume time on decorating your backside. I wonder why males do this on the other hand I am sure there must be some fact buried into it.

All I see was development from both corners; the body was same developed into a big fish now.

Several days passed, the journey with them was getting very good. I had no enough sorrows now because I knew Saba loves me, so I was finding a proper time to propose her. My friendship and mostly forthrightness with *Shaazu* was touching the sky, for times we would talk in secret regarding her. I was getting her bottom information through *Shaazu* that clearly showed she was totally disheartened which clarifies her profundity of love for me.

My frankness with *Shaazu* became the talk of the school and everyone admitted we were in love.

When reading a book one night I found another letter into it. I changed exultant; as expected it is Saba I said after seeing into the heavens with my eyes closed.

Without killing much time I start reading it crazily.

#My loving Sam

"The moment you laugh my heart would murmur to hug you very tightly. You are a flower who can make my life to blossom till my last breath. I don't know when I started loving you; you are the perfect match I was in search of. Your heart is transparent like a glass no impurities and no conservatism. I love you more than myself. Everyone knows that we are in love which is nothing but a rumor, come let's make it a reality. I need you very much. There is not any kind of need to me but I was lacking the true love, care and kindness which I hope you will give me. I don't want to meet you in person until your reply comes. Please write me back, and keep it in the same book I will collect it from there".

Yours loving........ Shaazu

What I read in the last, is it a mistake or a reality. I was startled. I kept mum for few minutes seeking divine help to clear me if it was a mistake or a reality. How could a girl fell in love with me who knows I love someone else? How could a girl fell in love with me who almost proposed for me to someone else? What the hell is going into this world? I had no feelings for her nor will it come I know. I had no right even to see other girls as my heart was kept my Saba. I really want to strangulate *Shaazu*, such a cheater. I think all of my hopes are shattered. I hated *Shaazu* for this. I thought to frame the response letter spiting my anger.

#Shaazu

"*I had heard girls are selfish thanks to you for becoming the example. I know you are my best friend and it will be enough good to keep it limited only to that. I swear to give up talking with you if you had taken my frank behavior otherwise. I don't love you nor will it happen till my last breath. There is only one sketch printed on my heart that is of Saba, the girl whom I really love the most since we met five years before. She is everything I prayed Allah to give me; I hope she also loves me back. I am totally hers from top to the bottom. She is not only the breeze of the dawn for me but she is my oxygen as well, so fresh and so innocent, I am made for her. I am ready to sacrifice myself for her I am not saying it but it is my promise. So hopefully you must have got the depth of my love for her. She is even my all time favorite human being. Forgive me if you think I was rude in this whole message*"

Sam.

I put the letter in between the same pages where from I got it.

I don't need to talk anyone in the class the following day, but if somebody wants I can. Saba is not even having a babies chat with me and *Shaazu* had done unexpected so no hopes for that day. I kept my bag into the class and went away so that *Shaazu* could pull the letter out. I don't need to keep a secret eye over my bag as I know it was *Shaazu*.

I came back after several minutes and found nothing; the letter was taken off.

The Saturday evening doesn't pass like last one; things were changing rapidly for me.

As usual I went to take the breakfast in the canteen Sunday morning, I ordered potato curry, had some place for the chair to sit in the open. I was done with one chapatti when my eyes fell on *Shaazu* coming to the canteen too. She greeted as usual and surprisingly there was no effect on her, she greeted me like she had done nothing and her behavior of talking was the same. I wondered and build a bad image of her into my mind. I was mum but she forces me to open my mouth.

Why you look so sad, she said.

No, I am fine, I said still focused my eyes on the potato curry.

Then what is wrong with you, she said.

Nothing I am okay only thinking what a horrible character girls have.

What happened? She asked me once again.

Don't you know? I gave a dirty look to her.

How could I know? Is everything alright?

Don't change the topic, I gloated her and really wanted to slap her hard. I wonder how she managed to be so frank with me behaving if she doesn't know anything.

Can you have a say? Sam.

Don't waste your time just order what you want and don't bother about the bill I said in rage.

What is wrong with you, she screamed.

I pulled out the letter from the pocket and gripped her.

Read and you will come to know. I said irately.

She read all and was shocked too.

I don't write it oh! My GOD I really don't know about this. I could see tears into her eyes. I know how much you love her, how is this all possible from my side; I swear I don't know all about this. You are my best friend who belongs to Saba I can understand your feelings and emotions, she loves you too. I don't know how to break hearts.

There was innocence into all what she said. I strongly believe you. I said.

She guessed who might have done that but found no one.

You open the letter and identify the handwriting. I said.

No, it is not Saba's handwriting, she writes clear and large she said after giving a deep look at the letter. There are hundred plus girls in our batch and 500 plus all over school how it is possible to get her on her handwriting.

Yeah it's too tough, but how to find her, I said.

Give the letter to me, I have some doubt on this issue I will come with the answer tomorrow. She said.

Okay, I said.

There is ninety nine percent of probability of gotten it written by some another girl by Saba, she is smart and witty moreover she must be checking me. I said.

May or may not be. She said.

She shouted but I paid the bill, as expected.

We rushed to our respective hostels, it was Sunday, and my fellows were still kissing the quilts.

I opened the door and entered in as quietly as I could start thinking about this all. If it is Saba then I deserve to give a party off course yes.

Time went by; neither the letter nor *Shaazu* came back with the answer. But whole scenario was changed after that.

Saba who was crushed with my comments earlier about my love start building close relations with me, I don't know why meanwhile I am in puzzle thinking about the letter.

Another couple of days went by, I could hear some voice from the other cabin in central library it was enough time passed with them to get their voices it was Saba and *Shaazu* talking and laughing, I preferred to listen whatever they are gossiping about. I could hear Saba saying, *"it was my plan to write him that letter to get if he love somebody or not, the depth of his love for me could be clearly imagined from his writings, he was very straight in his reply, he is very loving. I am quite happy you don't know how much I like him, I want him right now, he is very simple, kind and charming, yeah he is little silly in studies but he will get trained, no issue for that, even I will also help him. He loves me very much; everything I got from the letter was amazing and unexpected which make me cry. I got melted inside, he is so cute. Just check the letter and taste it you too."*

Her words amazed me, such a trick and such a plan to make me talk the truth. I am not angry here but my lips got stretched to make my teeth visible. She was an all-rounder and that was the reason to start loving her more.

I extended my steps towards their cabin, I behaved if I know nothing, and the moment I got myself inside I could see *Shaazu* hiding something behind her. I knew what it was, obviously the letter.

What you are doing here, I asked.

We were reading newspaper, they said, but I couldn't see any paper in front of them.

Saba invited me to have a chair besides her and I accepted only for five minutes which spend mostly eyes into eyes as *Shaazu* was not comfortable I decided to rush out for my hostels.

Saba approached me frankly now, and I know the cause. She calls me the favorite human being which ever met her, we are yet to propose and it wouldn't be wrong to say it was a love without a proposal, it happens never. We know everything even I know she was waiting for my proposal. But I didn't. I thought to show her who I was in reality and what kind of guy I am, so that it couldn't be a hurdle in our relationship. I controlled my heart waited for some days to be spent with her like a friend.

Saba was enough witty to manage to spend most of time with me, because she knows everything was done but I still tried to behave if I am yet to get who had written the letter.

I want to spend some days with her like a friend and nothing more than that, we spent several days and came to the conclusion I would never get such girl to love me that much, she really cares of me not for my health but of my money as well, she was a girl who never liked me to buy something for her in those several friendship days, it was first time in the history I met such girl. She had a transparent heart as well. She was ten times beautiful inside than that of outside.

My heart is burst as we know we love each other even she is waiting to get my proposal; I decided to propose her, again by writing a letter. There was no need of pigeons or horses unlike ancient times. I sat in the arm chair gifted by my mom, to write the most beautiful lines for her which we both had been waiting for years.

#My Saba

I always wanted this day to come and hit my heart again and again so that I could see you to add years to my life. You kept your image in my heart since the day we met some six years before when we both were kids. I have never seen such simple and beautiful girl like you. I loved you then to keep me living, I love you now to get you and I will remain loving you to keep you alive to love me to make my life worth living. The past years were simply very tearful, my mind was full of thoughts for you and it is quiet unexpected that such coincidence brought us closer once again. Perhaps even our creator has some ideas to grow us the beautiful love birds ever. I love you very much and I promise to stay with you even after our demise. My heart does something different it's in me beating for you to keep me alive. I love you.

Yours forever
Sam

5

❦

The relationship starts With truth

#My Sam

    I don't love you, I just hate you. It's early. Why did you Took lot of time to say this, wasn't I beautiful? Don't you know how impatiently I was waiting this moment? I love you. It wasn't only your right to fell in love with me when we firstly met but it was me who got lost in your heart forever as well. I love you and I am blessed to get loved by you. My happiness couldn't be measured in units I am simply frightened that this happiness shouldn't become the reason to my death. Let me to start our relationship with a truth. That day the letter was sent by me and your response changed my eyes into waterfall, I am sorry for that but it was my necessity as the situation never let some another option for me to do. I love the way you loved me in your previous letter, you are my reason to live and I am your atmosphere.

Yours every time
Saba

I punched my fist into the air. We were in love already but this response letter was some authentication and license to touch her romantically. I loved the truth she spoke first up, that gears our relationship towards honesty, understanding and success. It was a new experience going to examine both of us; we were innocent faces entering into the beautiful world. I took this step as a big challenge in my life. People did usually say, love breaks and destroys the career and dignity of lovers, but I was totally opposite to it. I don't think so; it merely depends upon how you behave. I even had examples of those who loved and failed in their lives. But they never became an issue to me.

It was new life beginning, a life which was not known by us, a life which can make us or break us, a life full of love and care and a life unforgettable.

Most people would admit it a wrong time to get into love because the preference was to develop our career first; she had a dream to become a doctor while mine was to become a writer. For us it was love without knowing its consequences but our courage, faith, truthfulness and understanding was enough strong to give us confidence, we could do wonders but who cares about these things when love enters his mind.

After some days we met in the corridor. She felt shy and dropped her head down; I had a clever smile over my face.

Hello, have a pleasure to look into your Sam's eyes; I said carefully looking her silky hairs.

I love your name, she said with her head still hanging of shyness.

That means you love my name only? I said.

Yeah! She looked into my eyes came forward and gave me a tiny slap, saying, it is the punishment because you did it late. I love whole of you plus your name.

Even Saba is the most beautiful name, I too love it, but to be frank I love this name because it's your name and your case would be the same that is for sure, is that?

Hahahahaha....Absolutely, Names always do make an image; don't bother about yours its good. She said.

But your image is not bad you fish, you big fish, I said.

My name is not fish my dear. I don't know why you nicknamed me this.

Leave it you won't get it, it is enough complicated.

Tell me, please.

See, but before I could speak up you had to promise not to slap me. I said.

Okay, I will not.

See, it's a nick name for you, it's my own discovery and nobody knows what its meaning is. You have got his name for your body physique. I replied.

She laughed as loudly as she could. How creative it is, and laughed again. You look very dangerous, I am afraid. But I wonder why you couldn't study if you had got a mind sharper than me. She said.

It's nothing like that, you are genius, and I hope you would teach me all subjects except English.

I will, promise, and remember you had told me that you would teach me English for that isn't it? She said.

Oh! Really I could remember, I said.

Sam, what do you want to be? She asked.

Simply a father to your children, I said and we burst into laugh.

Hahahaha…..oh! Hahahaha oh! Oh! You are really a bad boy.

What is your aim? I asked the same question waiting if she would give some different answer.

I want to become a good human being; she said and laughed hahahahaha.

Sam, I want to become all yours this time that time every time forever. I don't know how to break hearts nor I want to get mine broken. I am simple girls who love you madly, I want to be yours from top to bottom and I want to die before you, I think we should make some promises before we could start our new life.

Saba, you are the lady I love the most on earth.............
Stop ....

I want your hand over my head before you could say anything, she said.

I got my hand over her head slowly and start saying...

I promise I will marry you.
I promise not to deceive you.
I promise never to lie to you.
I promise to keep you happy.
And I promise never to let you down.
I promise to keep all my promises.

Now it is our turn. I said.

She kept her hand over my head, and start saying....
I promise to be obedient.
I promise to love you till my last breath.
I promise to do anything to get ourselves married.
I promise to be truthful.
I promise to teach you. (Smiles)
I promise my promises include your promises.
And I want to die before you.

It was getting late but the feelings were getting deep for each other, the promises gave some confidence to me and it gave me courage and guarantees to live with each other forever.

I went to the hostel start reading after dinner unlike before. The day you are happy you eat less but do your work with some extra energy. Yet I was not getting the calculus on the physics book and the reactions in chemistry they seem all beamers, the easy questions in mathematics seem a river to drown into and the miscellaneous was if I was illiterate, I couldn't even read what the question says how to treat with it.

I closed the book but never gave up, I thought is there any chapter which I could understand and soon I opened another option the biology and switched to the reproduction chapter.

I was changing into genius, I start getting everything with ease, everything written was genuine even I personally know some facts written. I understood some images related to me but I couldn't even think of others, because poles need holes to stand erect in the ground. Something written was already inbuilt so no need to read the theory. I jumped to another page and could see some pictures. I never get the sketch except one image. That time I firstly came to know that even publisher's are misers for not using enough colored ink on the images to get them clearly.

I closed the book and approached Saba next day; we selected a half noticed place where we could teach each other, we sat down to start the proceedings and all I could hear was…

Hey! Sam what the hell you are doing here, you don't know the rules and regulations of this institution.

Rotated my neck approximately 160 degrees to find he was the peon, it is very irritating when somebody would insult you like this in front of your girlfriend.

I asked him if anything was wrong in that. I even explained we use to study from each other.

No, not at all for this you need to get permission from the principal sir.

I asked if it was a crime.

Get lost from here you both, and you depraved, get lost, pointing to Saba.

Hey you fuck. To whom you did call all this, tell anything to me you want, I cannot tolerate even a single word against her, I will strangulate you, I jumped and choked him meanwhile my Saba came to separate us.

Tell your names and classes, I will go and complaint to the chairman.

What can you do, go I don't mind.

Saba remain biting her nails, she scolded me over this.

I planned to report the principal before he could complaint, Saba agreed.

We both went to the principal quarter and put into words all what happened. Principal Sir meanwhile called the peon.

Sir, I am very weak in studies so I approached the topper of section A to train me in difficult subjects.

Aren't there the teachers for you?

Yes sir, but she belongs to my own region, I teach her English and she teaches me rest of the subjects. That is it sir.

And why you argued with him, isn't he twice of your age? Why you behaved him like this? He said pointing towards the peon.

Not only argued but he abused and even slapped me, the fucking peon said.

That is your biggest gaffe, you just call your parents, both of you, and I want both of you to be kicked out of this institution.

Firstly we want to send a letter to their homes in order to get their parents here, he talked himself.

Saba, start weeping ferociously, I could see tears into her eyes, for what Saba is being punished.

I pulled out my handkerchief and start wiping her tears. Principal is seeing all this.

Sweetie… I am here I won't allow it to happen. I said while cleaning the tears out.

Jaanu, I couldn't bear this all, my father would die after knowing her daughter was roaming with other guys in the hostel. She was sobbing.

I am here nothing will happen my sweetie, I promise, I will not let it to happen.

Sir, please leave Saba, teaching one another and sharing knowledge is not a bad thing, I expect you to set her free. I said.

Are you rescuing her, and any special cause behind it? He said looking at me angrily.

Yes sir, we both are innocent, we didn't a crime. She is a girl sir, I know her dad he would kill her, you are also a father you should know the value of female dignity and honor, and I beg you to please don't make her to go mad anymore.

Saba looked at me surprisingly.

Perhaps she doesn't believed what I was asking to principal sir.

What happened sweetie? I asked her.

Her name isn't sweetie it is Saba. Principal Sir was trying to correct me.

Keep mum don't you hear she also told me *Jaanu (my life)* before this, I mumbled that never reached him. I thought inside.

I apologize, sir. I said in a soft temper.

At last principal sir agreed to liberate her after warning her not to indulge in such kind of activity.

I filled my lungs with lots of oxygen. Thanking the creator.

You go now sweetie, I said.

No how can I go without you. I will not. She said.

My sorrows were only mine and they would destruct me a lot but today if it approaches it got shared and destructed itself because I am in love. My mind framed this thought.

Don't take any pain regarding me; I will be okay my sweetie, I will do something to get me free only if you would go from here.

But promise you will tell everything what they did with you.

Ok my dear I promise.

He called my father, he came and I was suspended for three days.

Nobody in my home talked me because they had been told that I was caught with a girl during night.

Everyone started commenting against me, it was India, most of time I cursed not to be born in European countries where even reality is grounded on the other hand our culture and society is framed in a way where even rumors effects more than realities, it was a case of love so nobody would pardon me it was for sure.

Had it Being any case of corruption, rape, murder and thievery I would have been pardoned that time itself. This was the equation of our country where love is admitted the biggest crime mighty than rape and murder.

Three days after I was back, I told Saba everything and as expected she couldn't hide her tears.

She told me not to come closer to her because this issue may change the doubt of the students into reality, we were in love it became as common as atoms.

I don't accept her, but there was no option other than to avoid our lectures. I was sure if I couldn't study carefully for the rest of two months I would get failed. As in our societies eleventh class is considered very simple but we can know its value.

A notice made me read about the chairman of the school who was going to visit the institution in few days, I planned to seek some help from him, and maybe he could allow us to study together. Our classes would go off at sharp 4pm producing no possibility to study there.

I didn't studied five days till chairman came, I wrote a letter to him regarding his issue, he was a broadminded personality, he not only allowed me but appreciated as well.

We are granted permission; nobody can now talk against us. We can even find a place much safer than the earlier one. We had the license to study in open as well.

Saba couldn't believe this had happened, she remained calm over this case, we chose our place, there were noticed, half noticed and fully unnoticed places where we could study. We could change them according to our needs I hope you got it.

As expected we preferred the noticed place for initial days to show off.

After days we went to half noticed places to practice the mathematics, physics and to study chemistry reactions and had some good times with each other as well.

She taught me all the subjects there and I used to teach her English. Every day we used to visit twice there, one in the morning for one hour to teach her English before the class could start and other in the evening for at least two and half hours where she would teach me rest of subjects.

I would come to the hostels and would revise all that; she made me to work hard and used to give me good amount of homework.

She changed me into an innocent guy, I would never talk of romance to her but I only focused on my target. The attitude to marry a doctor in future came up with enough sufferings, hard work and courage in me. The tailor master would feel it cheap if her daughter argues to marry a person who doesn't know anything. It was best choice to divert myself from kisses to hard work. I have to become something special if I want to marry her otherwise it would be very tough.

My marks got increased like a bamboo tree.

I use to study more, and each day we would test each other that developed us.

The phobia of reading was gone out of me now, the teachers especially the physics sir would call me his favorite students and thanks Saba for that, I strengthen my image into his eyes.

We were improving through each corner, my marks, presentation skills and my repo would increase continuously and even she start getting good marks in English as well.

The first year passed on good heights for both of us. She topped the class in the finals and I was second which promoted me to join section "A" with her. It was not enough we continued our routine the same for the most important year of our life. The twelfth standard...

Gashuuuu.....Saba changed into *Gaashu,* I loved her very much so I named her *Gaashu* (the light of my eyes)

Ghashu..... Please show me a problem, we had test the following day.

We had done it already ok don't bother come and sit.

I sat opposite to her. I opened my rough book and got the perfect explanation from her.

Any more problems, she said.

No. But I want to teach you English this evening it may be I can't come tomorrow morning because of the class test.

Ok, my sweetheart, I loved that word for me.

As planned we choose the fully unnoticed place

I opened the book and got myself ready to teach her.

I was explaining the models and clauses.

I would get exited on each time viewing her; she was dressed in pink all over. Her face looked like a marigold. Her medium sized pink lips seem inviting mine when she would utter some word. Her smile was attracting with all the leveled white teeth visible.

I didn't paused even the chapter was finished.

Jaanu the chapter is finished, she told me. Now our each and every sentence to each other started with the beautiful words *Jaanu* and *Ghaashu*. I call her *Ghaashu* and she calls me *Jaanu*.

Stay for some time, I said in a little voice.

It was a chill November evening, surroundings went darker and darker, and the dogwoods start their job. The insect's start smacking our faces while smaller ones tried to enter into the eyes. Darkness dominates everywhere, I came closer to her, put my hand on her shoulder and start disturbing her hair from behind. I got red cause it was my first attempt to do so. She was not comfortable with all this she wanted to leave and I remembered she had called me dangerous one day which might be a reason but I know she is really connected me this time. I pulled her scarf and placed it on the ground, her curly hair would disturb her face before she start helping them behind her ears I too joined her to take some advantage, she was getting late to her hostel but I don't want to lose that opportunity. I whispered *I love you* into her ears and she does the same adding 'too' to that sentence. She looked simply beautiful, I looked into her eyes and start biting my lips and disturbed her cheeks with my right hand, her lips were glittering and wet inviting mine to be over them for several time. I came closer and put my lips on hers, my debut kiss to any girl having intentions drowned into romance and enthusiasm. I had no experience how to kiss but besides that our nose disturbed us little bit. I was having lots of excitement, taking full benefit of the darkness and of the November evening that was very chill which would bring us more closer to get warmth. I laid her horizontally on the ground very keenly with chest upwards. I got myself on her fully start sucking her face and lips amorously. She could murmur it is enough but I still went to climb on her stomach, I tried to pull her pajama but it was hard to pull it down, she was gone very deep in excitement, I sucked her stomach and licked her chest very much for several minutes my sexual parts were proving more dangerous, I sucked her again from top to the navel. I turned from another side and got the smoothest and fleshy part as my prey. I rubbed her chest I whispered one more sentence into her ears *'remove your clothes'* she didn't respond as I pulled her sweater out she was unconscious and my breathe was going fast in and out if I was climbing the Mount Everest, I again whispered the same words into her ears after removing my shirt but she never replied. I was eager to do sex. I became wild and pulled her pajama which shattered due to my giant force. Oh! Fuck the pajama got a cut at unnecessary place even I was so wild to try something from there but the milestone was afar. It had been thirty minutes till. I begged her to remove the clothes for first and the last time but she ignored. I hugged her very tightly and fell loose soon. I got relaxed still on her lying horizontally. I got up to put on the dresses including her. We saw each other and smiled she slapped me with smooth hands proving I was very wild and dangerous.

The night was enough darker now and the watch showed 6: 21 pm. Informing a full romance for thirty five minutes.

Oh! What the hell, the main hostel gate would be closed. She shouted.

Nothing will happen. I said.

The warden would ask some stupid questions before I could go inside, what to do.

I could see some lights functioning in the dispensary and we moved towards it.

It was medical ma'am distributing some medicines and Saba also entered to get some medicine for fake common cold.

Even ma'am doesn't examine her she was in a hurry as the dinner time for girls was getting closer. She only managed to pick some tablets to handle Saba. It was not important to check if the medicine was correct, it was only a gate pass for her, first time in my life I saw people using medicine for some purposes which even hadn't a micro link with that.

We were about to depart, ma'am called Saba to wait so that they could go into the hostel together.

I looked at Saba and smiled because her problem was over. I got double happiness. I said her good night and went off.

The next day we couldn't see into one another's eyes. We got introverted; I managed to quit a place where she could have easily seen me, it was my exam day the paper was very easy but some of the class mates could be seen copying, I read things that was the reason I was able to do what paid me after the results. I topped the class in some subjects and I became eager to top in the finals.

Oh! It is getting too late; I don't want to become regular from punctual, Saba would be waiting. I rushed outside and ran till I reach there.

Hi...She responded without eye contact.

Look into my eyes, my sweetheart.

Just quit from here and take my pajama to the tailor to get it sewed.

Ok I will, but that wasn't my fault.

Pulling my pajama like a tiger isn't your mistake? She said with a sweet innocent smile on her face.

Ok. My sweetheart I will get it repaired, but what would I tell whose this is.

Leave it, I was joking, I had already kept it to recollect that worst night.

Was it a worst night my sweetie? I questioned if I was acting into some movie.

No, my *Jaanu*, it wasn't, thanks to the tailor who had sewed that pajama otherwise it wouldn't had been possible for me to get up from the bed for at least two weeks. She said and I burst into a loud chortle. She accompanied.

Sweetu… are we going to study. Don't be confused what the character is, it is only the loving name she called me with.

Yeah! But let's gossip for some minutes more. I said.

Oh! Hoo! Hooo… not at all, you mean to eat up time so that you can repeat what you did yesterday. I don't want to get my ribs broken today, she told into a childish tone. If you want we can start now, otherwise you may leave.

What, Romance? I said.

Stupid, idiot, I mean study. She smacked my thigh.

Hahahaha ok let's start my *Ghaashu,* (the light of my eyes) I said.

It was mathematics as per the timetable.

We solved some tough questions and the miscellaneous exercise as well. They were long but quiet interesting. I was happy to start our relationship in a descent and professional way, I never consumed much time over other activities what couples do but sometimes it becomes compulsory to practice some romantic shots after all we are humans. We had some better understanding right from the first point. I caught her good things and she caught mine perhaps the only one I had, I had limitations limited to infinity and my talent was limited to one which was my English skills.

We worked hard on our limitations as love was a challenging thing, we don't let ourselves down, off course it becomes difficult to manage all things when a new element is added to your time table that was our love, we need time to think for ourselves, we need enough time for that, we need to talk with each other and mostly the inclusion of love into our routine make our nights quiet short. I wasn't able to sleep to my full because of her thoughts and dreams, obviously same was the case with her.

Half of the night was consumed by lovely dreams and half was consumed by the cats and rats making clatter throughout the whole night. I had experienced several things common in hostel life, cats, dogs and rats stood at top. Their sounds *accumulate* 50% of our hearings per day.

The morning chill wasn't willing to get me to open my eyes, but what to do when I had to teach English to my favorite human being. It was getting very chill and according to weather forecast Kashmir will receive snow fall in many of the areas included Srinagar.

The examination time was approaching; we had 100 percent preparation credit goes to her only. We would meet and talk continuously any place; the preparation leave or we can say summer vacation comes into action leading everyone to stay in the hostel to get prepared.

People don't have enough work to do in winter, the snow was falling and soon it covered the ground, the world looked white. The vehicles could be seen having chains surrounded to the tires. None others the winter totally belong to the children who never felt cold nor they had to keep something that could make them feel warm. Children always loved the whiteness as they could make unlimited things out of snow; they could make a snow man to play with and could even make different winter ice creams by adding sugar, milk, coffee and chocolates with the snow. The birds would disturb your bedrooms and roofs they even go to make a nest on the cupboard in your bedroom. Their shelters are shattered; the snow can't be a thing to bring happiness for everyone. The most loved moment in snow is when you would get lots of snow dust over your body when you would walk under a tree. The trees would become obeisant to the ground, they are heavy of wetness and the weight of the snow make them bow to the ground, it look if the trees are begging the ground to unload its innocent thin and weak twigs. Old people keep themselves very warm, they even don't go outside. The population looks if it is reduced by 50 percent, majority who would go to experience the falling snow are only and youth and the children and do maximum work in winters. The voice would not go anyway; it is too difficult to shout as your voice will surround you itself. Children would visit to the slopes or hilly areas so that they could take the savor of snow sliding. Adults could start snow fighting by standing meters afar to pelt snow balls on each other. Children's had no tools for that except a big polythene sheet which they use to place under their hips to get slipped from the slope. Everyone wants Kashmir be dressed white more and more after each passing years.

The march started on a good note. I attempted 99 marks in mathematics our first paper.

My entire exam went kissing the heavens as I attempted 95 to 100 marks for each of the subjects and it would be wrong not giving full credit to my dream girl Saba. A boy who had lost hopes even to pass the exam was predicting himself to be in the topper list. Everyone was packing their luggage; home is the beautiful place in this earth, so the entire world is beautiful for sure.

I told Saba to spend some time together in evening air and she responded affirmatively.

Ghaashu (the light of my eyes) how are you? I said after meeting her in the cold chill and rainy march evening.

I am fine, tell something new. She said.

The air was cold, slow winds start no insects were heard making different noises the night was very quiet with few stars into the sky. The trees would make swish by going both sides and the leaves were trying to come out. I had a cap on my head colored red and she had everything weaving into the air. The fast moving air was disturbing her; she always went to grasp her frock from her thighs to restrict its flying. The wind blew through her face and she kept her eyes half closed. I hold her hand and went under an apple tree to start our proceedings.

The snow had melted leaving the ground muddy, the tiny grass was little wet. I collected big polythene cut it into two to sit upon under the apple tree.

You know, to leave the institution is not a big issue for us we could be more practical in our residential areas. I said.

I know *Jaanu*(my life), but don't tell anyone about our relationship otherwise I am sure I couldn't survive.

I can understand.

I never wanted my parents should ever know about it, they would kill me if they did, they are very strict.

Ok, I am going to add one more promise to the promise list, I promise not to tell anybody about our relation. I said.

This is like my cute baby; she said and gave me a flying kiss.

Jaanu how much you love me? She asked.

That was the difficult question I could answer, it wasn't a question of chemistry, physics or any other subjects to have a definite and short answer, but it was a question which cannot get you feel satisfied after answering it even hundred times. Each time you would feel to add some more to the answer to make it more impressive, loving and attractive. I didn't answer this question for some minutes.

What you are thinking about my sweetheart, she said very innocently.

Gaashu (the light of my eyes)..... I can't answer your question it is difficult one, I only know I can only answer its fraction after all the water bodies would turn into ink to write continuously for seven more generations. I simply want to die while writing about the qualities you possess.

Oh! *Noooooo*...She put her right hand over my lips to get my words clogged. Idiot, how many times should I tell you not to say rubbish; she made her face and slapped me with her eyes wide open.

Ok, my dear I am sorry, I said.

Jaanu (my life) don't you know how much I love you. My life without you is impossible; don't talk anything bad about yourself. You are the prince of my dreams and I am the princess of your imaginations.

I liked her sentence; I thought to put her in the same question she asked me, I hesitated at first but managed to ask...

Jaanu (my life) how much you love me?

More than you, she didn't thought much and replied quickly.

Her answer was very wise and I was beaten, every time she would add one to what I did tell.

She was a girl of some inbuilt talents and I was sure she would make it to acquire great heights one day; she demonstrated her extraordinariness in every department.

We had no time to go immersed into that night in any ways. The time was little so I preferred to share a romantic good bye kiss, I pulled her close to me but she went back and start reciting some words I couldn't hear nor could understand but I was sure she was praising that I shouldn't go wild. We don't sit unlike last time, and we started our job standing still. Her body was enough warm perhaps dozen degrees warmer than the normal body temperature. Who was going to care about it all, I went to hug her very tightly and felt the same things as before, her hair was wet I could feel, I kissed each section of her face very hard. I wasn't shy at all.

Everyone was jumping in joy, and the cutest time in your life is when you are finished with examinations. No one wants to let the gossips pass, everyone would remain waiting the farewell party some boys could dance, some could sing all night and some could do different things.

After the dinner, all of us got crowded in the seminar hall. The moment we made entry all the students and teachers gave a standing ovation. Lots of decorations were crafted sensationally; Saba was dressed like an orange, again her physique became prey to my eyes. I gave her a flying kiss and so did she. I could see cold drinks and different kinds of fruits and other eatables placed in different corners. Big gifts were packed to be distributed. Our juniors had done really well to make it the unforgettable day for all of us. The music system was amazing and the lightening system was supreme. Students were going to be awarded for their performances throughout the entire year. We sat in a queue behind the teachers. The party starts with a farewell song beautifully composed.

The sofas were decorated with balloons and all that, we got served with banana shake first up and then the grand night went on with an inspiring speech from the principal sir. He talked about several success stories and gave some valuable suggestions thanks to my perception which got changed over the months otherwise I was a boy who would have asked about success shortcuts.

The music starts with gorgeous dance. Some plays were their related with love and affection and success.

The game section was very interesting; teams were made to take challenge for consuming anything in some given time, it was some chicken pieces to be swallowed in three minutes as I was already famous topping the list my name was called and everyone started hooting. I got up shook hands with the competitor who started after the bell struck third time. He finished the chicken leg with some other pieces in four and half minutes. Now it was the turn of the biggest meat eater, I tapped my stomach till the bell struck three all the students started roaring, I never mind if it was something hard coming my way even boons found their way direct into the throat. Hopefully I won by one minute.

Time to drink something, not me, the competitors were already there, how many of you think it would be vodka or beer, I am sorry it was milk and juice drinking competitions, delighted to see that much talent hidden into the students who can gallop anything coming into their ways. Not students but they looked the ships of desert consuming the water like bulky Arabian camels. The night was going on cold nine. I rotated my neck around and found teeth everywhere, fully thirty two times more than the faces. We were called to speak something about anything on the dice, easily guessing, everyone was going to comment richer, hundred percent. Everyone gave richer comments as about the school and produced whatever they want to be, if anybody does hate I was sure he or she is going to tell enough good than rest. The same thing happened as predicted, one of my close friends who never liked the strictness and workload of the school gave splendid comments and highlighted only those things which he hated.

My eyes could see my life getting up, and I became attentive. Going to listed and understand it all wow!!!

Good evening different dignitaries' and all the people around me. I never want to leave such place that made me what I am today but we have to. I have no words to thank almighty who at last heard my prayers and gave respect to my tears. He brought something in my life and how immediately that became my reason to live. I found my milestone here which would have been a dream for me if not preferred this school. It's very valuable to spend your life with such individuals who made your life worth living and changed your destinies and fortune.

Her speech was over, and everyone roared and clapped but it was only me who got her speech perfectly, the thing she talked about was me and nothing else.

All were done; it was the time to get the awards for best performances of the year both in sports and academic fields.

Principal Sir was on the dice.

The last but not least, it was a wonderful journey with all these students who did a condemnable job for the success of this institution. They showed their performance in each and every field, whether it was sports, academics or other. My throat is getting clogged to step forward; I don't wish them to leave this institution. But I have to. A student is never made by forcing him to read books only, books only can't build a student but the major part goes to the sports department who works on the students to maintain their fitness, to reduce his tension, to refresh him, to get him both mental and heartily exercises. All are the things by which a student can get a maximum pick up, and can read and write effectively and efficiently. Without sports and mental exercise education is blind. Our faculty team had selected some students who had done really well in the maximum sections so let's distribute the awards to them.

Its *Mania* madam presenting, the best performer in academics and it goes to SAM.

All was cheers from every corner. It was a dream award for a boy who had come here to fail only but time talks itself. How things get changed no one knows. I was very happy I hold the award kissed and got emotional. I announced to dedicate this award to Saba without whom it would have been only a dream for me. It was very hard to outclass such swift student in every field but I was dedicated I can do it; I never went with the plan thinking that she isn't brilliant which produced the key to my success. I always pointed out her secrets behind her success, she was able to do math and physics in seconds that was nothing but hard work which had took her to that stage.

Other students got some awards and there were lots of cries out, enough hooting and cheers.

Now it is time to give the best writer of the year award and it goes to Miss Saba, outclassing Sam in the field.

Again it was a wonder happening, a girl who was brilliant in every subject except this one finally outclassed her teacher and this is called success. Saba went smiling to receive the award she kissed it like me and announced she is dedicating it to me. I was extremely happy over our successful journey.

Now, it is the time to give the best sports person award and it again goes to Mr. Sam, principal sir was roaring.

It was genuine to get this one, quiet happy with two awards at the end of the night, so this one goes to my parents who never stopped me from playing cricket.

Principal Sir went to announce the winner of another award.

All the students had done extremely good to get those awards, but toppers cannot be plural. We had two students in the list to give this award for but unlike in the best writer award the equation got reversed here. What it could be? Any guess? Principal Sir asked. But nobody came up with the answer. Saba smiled as she got the answer, I got it too that I am a looser this time.

Time to give the one and only supreme award….. It is *Mr. Ishtiyaq sir* to give student of the year award and again it goes to Miss Saba, beating Sam in the competition. Principal Sir got pumped up and he was roaring her name like a lion.

What it was happening was really out of expectations, if anybody would say about success I was sure to give this as an example. But only we people knew how we had acquired it all, what we hadn't done to get all this. I was in high spirits after receiving four major awards that day, and it wouldn't be wrong to say that whole of the years belonged to us only. That day I came to the conclusion *love never spoils it can build up persons having uncontaminated thoughts.* The party was over I found myself into back my room after I had an innocent kiss on Saba's beautiful hands.

We woke up early in the morning, the happiness doesn't allow me to sleep whole night, even I wasn't able to dream about somebody, but I did with eyes open. My parents arrived to take me at 10am; the distance from our place to Srinagar is 100 plus kilometers, thanks my father to present himself at a decent time. I greeted my father; he hugged me and kissed my cheeks.

We talked for a while before he would get the out pass.

I got changed, and got ready to leave. I visited everyone's room before I could do so; I hugged each other and start crying to lose my best friends. But everyone was helpless these things happen in life and you have to pass through these stages.

Papa…there is a girl from our area here; she is in my class.

Where is she?

Hostel

Isn't she going home?

Yeah, her father is coming.

Ok it's good but I think we haven't enough time to meet her because I have some important official work; we need to depart as soon as it could be.

Ok. Let's go.

We had to walk till the main gate.

As soon as I reached the girls hostel, girls could be seen rushing in and out. I remain staring on the hostel from roof to the base but didn't found her. I stepped forward and looked back for the last time; I rotated my neck and saw Saba on the top floor weaving her had to say bye included some romantic flying kisses. I could understand from her gestures that she was insisting me to do the same but I was puzzled what to do when the world's number one strict father was besides me. There was no way to get my father's attraction and eyes diverted to some other thing that could prove some chance for me to offer her a flying kiss. I start taking little steps while pointing towards the administration block opposite the girls hostel so that his attention may get diverted.

Papa, this is our administration block. I said to make his neck to some rotation.

He rotated his neck quickly which means I gave my Saba a flying kiss too and waved my hand to say her good bye.

She laughed wildly after I did this trick. She weaved her hand and said good bye for the last time.

6

At Home

Once we got into our homes the situation took a turn. Indian parents would never allow their children to go outside without a reason, especially the law is meant for girls but in Kashmir the case is something different. Parents here never allow daughters to go outside in the day time without any reason if they did she is accompanied by some other friend or relative. Boys are looked after very seriously no parents would ever want their son to roam outside unnecessary, no parties and no hangouts. On the other hand nights are same for each gender; no boy or girl is allowed to step outside the main gate.

One day I managed to tell my mother to go to *Bumhama* it was nothing but Saba's village. She allowed me only when I said my cousin was also coming with me. I went alone; Saba had told me earlier that her house is pink colored double story building at the edge of the main three way road. I could see a house of same characters a girl on the staircase reading something. As I went nearer I identified she was my life Saba. I composed a lovely whistle which forced her eyes to see me. She was overwhelmed and tried to speak something which I never got. A little female kid was seen revealing from her house and she innocently told me, Sister is telling to wait in the ground. These words dropped on my heart like a cool breeze. On asking the baby who she was she innocently replied... *Sadat*, and went away.

I stepped towards the ground and saw no one there, the only thing I could see was cattle and the dense popular and willow trees surrounded it; it was a nice place to meet no one could see us.

Saba was seen coming with *Sadat*; she did greet me so did I as usual.

How was your journey my sweetheart, she said.

It was fine but I wasn't feeling good, everything was nice but I really don't want to travel with my father.

Why?

It looks odd paying attention to the Indian romantic songs when your parents are besides you.

Hahaha It happens with me as well.

Leave it now, how are you *meri jaan* (my life)

Yeah! I am fine but I suffered from common cold and cough in the initial days here.

Are you feeling well now, yeah?

Yeah I am feeling good, and no need to bother about.

I am always with you my sweetheart, please do inform me whenever situations start getting worse for you, my voice proved much innocence.

I am also with you *Jaanu* (my life) you just take care of yourself, if you are happy that means I too am happy, she said with enough flexibility into her voice.

It is very difficult to love in villages everyone has different perceptions and thinking, I am sacred to get seen talking you here, I said with little hesitance.

Off course, let the results be declared both of us will join the same college until have patience otherwise conditions may become worse. She said.

I can understand I know how to get things around. How I can wish us to be caught into some hardship, I said lovingly.

That is like my loving husband, she jumped on the top.

Husband?

Yeah! You are, any doubt?

I loved the way she uttered it, it was the best words I got to hear from her. I was very happy to hear all this. I didn't say anything for a minute the only thing I could do was smiling.

Why are you smiling I want answer from you and that is all. Aren't you my husband? Or you want to deceive me?

Oh my *Ghaashu* it's not like that how can you think about this all?

What is the problem, I think you are a gay. She said before bursting into a big smile.

Ha ha ha ha ha ha ha ha ha ha ha ha … we both laughed much.

I wonder what she told without any boundary we laughed loudly as my stomach was experiencing some pain inside.

How many children you want to have, I replied swiftly after hearing her earlier statement.

Thank God you are not what I thought; she said and makes me to laugh again.

It is the first time I had seen a girl like you, I said.

Yeah I know you had seen girls with beard, moustaches and horns, right?

Ha ha ha ha ha ha ha ha ha ha…Again she made me laugh until some water started coming out of my eyes, she joined me too.

It was the first time I could see happiness glooming into her face, her every organ was a proof of her simplicity, kindness, honesty and loving. My love for her was getting increased after every passing second. I wished I could fulfill all of her dreams and wants. I wished she could be happier with me after our marriage. This marriage was very far, we can make it provided to make our love be secret.

Don't mind my *Jaanu* (my life) I like to make others laugh and why not the person who is everything to me, she said in a gentle tone.

I was feeling out of this world talking to her so frankly, how one couldn't love a person madly who is able to do everything not for her but for you to get you satisfied. She was a girl to be loved million times more she was a face to be remembered till generations and a heart not to be liked but loved till the love ends itself. It was the finest afternoons I had ever come across.

For some time I wondered what love was all about, the much her innocence was exposed the more I became hers thank you to let me get love is always loved with hearts.

My heart refused to go home that day only to spend more time with her but we were helpless to take any action. I brought some cakes, cookies and other fruits to give her she refused to take before I could tell I will never show my face otherwise.

She went inside the main gate, in no time I could see her again on the staircase starring at me while biting an apple. I said her good bye and she followed me; I walked without seeing from where the road was my eyes were focused on to her from top to bottom. She was invisible hiding behind the trees and I went off with little steps.

In the evening I could see my father had brought an application form for journalism and literature because he knew I was good in English to build my career without taking my suggestion. Like every parent he also wanted me to become a doctor after my metric exams but I wasn't enough brilliant to obey his expectations. He called me in another room after we had dinner.

I have brought an application form for journalism so go with it. He said in low voice and added I never wanted you to become an English teacher in any primary school like me, but I had always thought to make you a skilled doctor who could save the lives of other people. I don't force you but you didn't make me happy today.

I didn't reply anything till he placed the form in front of me.

Fill the details its last date is closer, he said.

The twelfth class result was yet to get announced otherwise he would have got what I want to become but I managed to say. I don't want to read literature and journalism.

Then…then… are you going to become a doctor? He said harshly if he was insulting me.

Yes, papa my aim is to become a doctor and I will prove it.

He doesn't believe what I was saying and declared me mentally sick. I tried to convince him but he wasn't ready to agree because for him I was the same boy who had passed his science with divine help in the previous classes.

Papa I want to become a doctor now, I said again.

What? He touched my cheeks in delight and embraced me tightly and kissed my forehead.

Papa would you allow me to become a doctor now, I said emotionally.

Why not my dear son, I will even sell the fields to get to your aim but it needs percentage at least above 80, I think you can get it in your twelfth standard.

Papa, I will, I am sure.

He hugged me once again and appreciated me.

I became tight lipped and didn't say a word.

Saba was in her home and I was sure she must be following the routine. We never met for some time because her dignity and honor was everything for both of us. I never wanted to get her masked into hardships. I knew I was an inexperienced lover to grip all the things so I prefer not to meet to build situations terrible for her.

Two months later, I was reading a newspaper on the balcony my father came to me to ask my roll number once again. I guessed it might be my result.

My father went to the market to see the gazette; I could hear some noises into the kitchen downstairs. I could hear my father calling me.

I went down and he gave me a tight hug everyone was pumped up over my result, Sam had got 95.8% percent marks to top his school of over five hundred students.

My father reviewed the result tens of times to prove what he was seeing was right.

The only thing he could do to hug me very tightly with his eyes raining. I hadn't dreamt of it my son. What you had done is unthinkable and will remain untouchable for generations, he said with tears in his eyes. The father of a dull boy with a lazy nature was happy due to his son's achievement that he had predicted to sink down his status one day but the ship went to the opposite direction. Everyone in my house was surprised but happier. My mother thanked the creator in her own ways and father could be seen bowed in his prayers. It was the greatest moment in my family as no one had crossed the 55%% margin in the entire village till yet and no one had made it to pass higher secondary exams in my family. This news soon spread all over the village like fire. People could be seen coming in with gifts and different smiles. The people in our village had only two words into their minds to search for, one was fail and the other pass. If you have passed you are the most intelligent no matter how many marks you had secured. They even don't know what the term percentage was neither they do care for it. But this case was different people got a man who not only passed but got the highest marks and topped his school to bring three good news to celebrate for.

The same day, I got the newspaper with the toppers list, I was at the top with 95.8% and my Saba was second with 95.4%.

That night was something special for me as I was allowed to study doctoral. My father sold some land for my coaching from a very reputed coaching center. I was very happy to be allowed that will insist Saba to come for coaching to the same institution, before I could leave I thought to meet her once. I wrote a letter congratulating her for our success the letter was more loving than the content. I rushed out of my house it was raining; I kept the letter inside my pocket. The rain was becoming very dangerous but I kept my nerves tight. I reached near her house some way, every organ of my body was wet and dropping water drops. No one was seen at the staircase which could make me to wait for sure. I waited in the passenger shed for twenty plus minutes before I could see Saba going through the balcony, I weaved my hand and gestured to come out. She flashed into smile and soon I could see her coming out from the big metallic giant gate with something in her hand. No one was with her today, and no one was seeing near around. She ran towards me and I spread my arms to deposit her into my arms giving a smooth and lovely hug. She don't care I was wet as she got fixed with me if we were glued.

She congratulated me by adding "I am very happy that *mera ganda bachha (my bad baby)* made it to top the school" she wasn't happy for her achievement but for mine.

She was wet soon and forwarded the gift to me with gentle hands. It's a small gift for my sweetheart, she added.

I took it, not doing the mistake of thanking her; she would kill me if I do that.

I had nothing to give her except that letter that too half dry.

My sweetheart....I want you to join...............before she could say something further I stopped her.

I know what you are going to tell, I smiled and said.

What....what....what...

I know you want to tell me to join Sheikh Nour College for literature before you could tell I want to tell you one thing.

First of all tell me how did you get I am going to tell all this.

It's simple; you know I want to become a writer and for literature this college is best. I said.

How sweet my sweetheart is, correct guess, lots of kisses on your face and lips, she merely said it without doing it practically. I am very happy to be classmates once again, she added.

Are you mad my *Ghaashu*, how could we be classmates. I asked and smiled.

I knew she wanted to become a doctor so I had come here to tell her the happiest news that I had changed my interest from journalism to doctor, so we were going to be class mates once again by getting coaching from Bright coaching centre but she is getting happy for some other reason.

What you are thinking my sweetheart, she said with a smiling face.

Nothing, said I.

Then why you look if you are bewildered, she said with her voice going down.

I am going to tell you one another thing. I said.

Yeah I know what you want to say, she said in a hurry.

What?

You want to insist me to join Bright coaching centre for MBBS coaching because you know I want to become a doctor she said.

Yeah that is correct; I want you to get admission there and I thought to tell you so that you could be with me once again.

I can't take admission there, I have some other plans she said showing her teeth.

What plans, I don't want any, it's you who inspired me and made me worth to study medicals, how can I believe you had something else in your mind to do. I want to become a doctor my sweetheart.

Don't crack any comedy here, I can't believe you are going into some another field she said confidently.

I am not telling jokes, it's a reality.

I am again telling please don't tell this, I know you could be a good writer more over I don't know to call it a reality, a dream or success.

It's simple and please don't be so puzzled, said I.

I am not baffled over your case but I too have the same case like you, she said.

What case go for it, no more chatter, I said.

I am sorry I can't join MBBS, she said.

What?

Yeah I want to study literature to develop into a writer and whole credit goes to you, knowing you want to become a writer made me to say we could be classmates once again.

Was it a unity, a marvel, a surprise, a wonder, a success or anything else I can't give it a name, I got flummoxed to know both of us had transmitted and adopted one another's talents in such a way that changed our careers and fates.

This news inspired me very much and I thought love could make anything to happen by its strong affection. We changed the mentality, career, thinking, fate and lots more out of a thing which is treated badly.

There was no one around, the rain was at its business, our clothes were too wet her clothes got fixed on her body making her flesh visible from the transparent soggy frock, and her legs could be seen attracting whole of my eyesight. Her drizzling white face looked cute while a rain drop was hanging from her nose. It was a good kissing time, the rain had a great speed turning that evening to be more like a foggy morning and loosing opportunities in such circumstances was just like refusing a free lottery. And I hope everyone knows the next step. It was a kiss with a mighty taste, I don't kissed her as much as I drunk the water drops from all of her body.

We were done, and she said bye for the last time.

I too said her bye, and kissed for some seconds before we could leave.

Some days after I was send to the Srinagar to take coaching classes and she did fill her form to join degree college *Handwara* to study literature.

The MBBS exams were approaching, I went to home to take some praise from each corner and to be frank I went there only to meet Saba, I was sure that her prayers were enough strong to turn around anything.

The afternoon was little cloudy and I preferred to wait Saba at the bus stop. After some minutes I could see her coming out of a bus and came closer to me for a chat.

It was only three days to go to sit in the examination.

Hello my *Ghaashu,* how are you I said.

I am fine, and tell something about you, she said.

I came here to drink your prayers, you must know the exam is in next three days, said I.

Yeah, I know after I read the newspaper last night. My wishes are always with you. I believe you will crack the examination.

My sweetheart, do you pray for me ever.

Why not? I keep praying you all days and nights even I don't know when I fell asleep and your time table had always blessed me the scolds from everyone.

To hear she uses to pray me days and nights felt if I was in heavens and it adds when she told she is following my unique timetable.

Oh! Shit….

What happened?

Papa is here in the market and I am sure he saw us, I screamed.

I allowed her to go and I run away through the fields to reach my home. There was my mother who served me tea before I could hide myself in my bedroom. I was sure papa is going to take my class in the evening for this matter. In the evenings he called me and suggested only to focus about my studies rather to fell in any kind of activity which could be a cause of our contempt and insolence. If you do I would not care about your life. He did not agree what I said him to prove it was just a meeting with my ex-classmate. I left the place and went to my bedroom to prepare some chemistry reactions as I was a bit worried about them; the exam was over my head now.

Two days after I sat in the examinations, I did far better in every section but was not sure to be selected because it was an Indian examination where corruption had covered each and every thing. Seeing the past statistics of results I was worried to get selected, it was observed over the years that 80% of the selectees had rich fathers. I know the cause as well, I remember the day when our neighbor was caught red handed selling the MBBS question papers. All the information was not good for me because I knew I belong to such a family who couldn't afford to repair the broken mirror of our bathroom since two years. Getting selected on the monetary basis was a thing not to think of.

I opted to spend some days with my family till the result would come to whom I hadn't helped since years.

Our relationship was going smooth and it was still a secret between us even our kidneys and other organs weren't aware about it apart from heart. We met every day both in the morning and in the evening. I would wait her at the bus stop in the morning and the evenings to talk with her sometimes I went to her college in a proper uniform making sure not to get exposed. The MBBS result was only some day's afar when we planned to go on our first date.

My sweetheart I want to go to our first date, as you know MBBS results are coming anything could happen, and I have to stay in the city in both the conditions.

She put her hand on my mouth and doesn't let me to speak anymore.........

Don't speak rubbish, I hope you will make it to the selection list, I believe on my prayers. My worship and prayers will never go fruitless my *Jaanu* (my life) if it did I will believe I had never loved you with my heart, she said naively.

Sweetheart you don't answer to my question about the date. I said.

No need to go to the date, I think I can't come because my parents have to go to visit a doctor tomorrow morning I even can't go to the college I think.

Sweetheart it's a unity, my parents are also going in the reception party of my cousin brother tomorrow morning and they will be back after two days, It a golden chance for us to meet. I said.

Yeah, I have to go to meet my friend in your village; if I did I will meet you there surely.

That sounds good baby, I said feeling exited.

Next morning, my parents were getting ready; it was some fifty kilometers from our village so they left very early after

115

giving me lessons how to keep an eye over whole of the house. Our home was at the right side in the middle of a small street quiet unnoticed.

They left and I slept again respecting the routine, I made my mind not to open my eyes till ten.

Trin trin trin trin trin trin….. The clock was alarming, it was 9:59 my eyes were forced to open by the continuous noise of the clock, what the hell is? How could it happen a minute earlier? To spend one minute under the quilt is equal to 1000 minutes. But I kept that thought away only to bring another thought that Saba was coming to our village, with this I kicked the quilt meters away and got up like a spider man. I was ready; I took light breakfast and went to the terrace to see if anybody was roaming outside of my house.

I could see two girls entering that street that completes fifteen minutes for me on the terrace my eyes directly fell over Saba and it was a matter of some seconds to reach the main gate to welcome them. My Saba looked extra gorgeous in yellow dress, it suits when the face is white. They came close to me.

Oh my dear sweetheart, you are in time, I was waiting you to come I had already spent some time on the terrace to find you out.

Is this your home, she said.

Yeah, it is, It is three dozen years old, it is built when my father was yet to join the school.

It is very good, I like it.

I had seen, lovers would like anything of each other no matter how bad it is even the worst things seem enough good, same was the case with our home, its color was faded up from every part, the windows were the proof to get it was a old building, the roof was full of rust and the rooms had supreme ventilation system because maximum windows had glasses broken times before yet to get repaired the cause was only our studies. Knowing his income and necessities my father never spent money on other things except our studies. I said these words taking some time.

Her friend went away, she had some work somewhere leaving us alone standing in the street.

Who is in your home, she asked me in a very low tone.

There is no one except me, parents had gone to the reception party, grandpa and grandma are already there, brother has gone to Kerala to participate in the school level games and all sisters are in the school.

Why you went deep into the explanations, she said if she wants me something to say.

See, let's make our entry into my home, today is the golden chance for me to serve you, and more over you can see how ugly our home is inside, I said quietly.

She gave me a slap, no, I won't come, I know you will become dangerous and there is no one to help me except him, pointing her forefinger towards the sky.

Oh no…..I have no mood even to think about that today; please don't waste time come in, I requested.

She agreed and we got into our home for the first time this activity was never out of danger I knew we would be no more if anybody comes to know all about this but the probability for the danger was negligible. I locked the main door and went to my bedroom holding her hands firm.

Don't be so eager to know what happened next, I simply served her with tea, juice water and eggs, because I know the energy these items would provide was like a guest in her body.

We swallowed everything, it was not a time to discuss lots of things but it was something to utilize into much efficient and effective way.

I sat beside her and looked deep into her eyes for several minutes, her face was getting red and she looked a bit worried,

I knew the cause, all she would be cursing me inside but I also knew girls are also found of what was going to happen next. That moment my feelings were different than before, I felt something new in me for which I had most of hunger since the years. It was nineteen years without a single practical. I forgot all the biology books for a moment because the biggest and physical biology was in front of me getting crazy over each and every step. I got some sexual feelings inside but I put them away. I planned no to do anything except kisses and hugs. I started the proceedings; the prey was lying in front of a lion without eating it. I lied to do sex but she refused and warned if I did it she will shout. I took a look to whole of her body from top to bottom and felt electrified, my heart forced me to go wild and do whatever you want but my mind went totally against it and suggested me to be limited to kisses only. Though thinking and talking much doesn't look good when such beautiful face is lying horizontally in front of you eager to get disturbed. I was less experienced but I know skills can do the job and thanks I possess the finishing move to make girls unconscious, it was not the finishing move which the WWE superstars would use to win games for them but it was such finishing move which would finish the existence in the real world for a women for hours to drop them into the world of unconsciousness. It was nothing to do except pulling her towards me, she was opposing because she never wanted whatever my gestures and energy showed that time. I managed to lift her into my arms and laid her horizontally on my bed. She looked very beautiful in the dress, her dresses were more in number than me, I don't see but matured people could guess. I pulled out her sari and her brown curly hair was exposed. We came closer and had a kiss on our lips for longer time, that day there was enough time for us to do anything, I kissed her entire face before I could move towards the neck, I don't want to leave any corner of her body untouched not by my hands but by my lips, if I did that day I was the biggest coward in the world. I kissed her neck from both sides and she was going in the other world, but not yet. I was thinking inside about sex but thought against it several times, I was too a human like you I couldn't stop myself and started pulling her frock out but she went against it which proved she wasn't gone yet. I kissed her much more from both corners of her chest and face she dropped her arms wide spread on the bed if she was dead, I checked her consciousness by pulling her frock once more, she didn't move, I got she was gone. Mission completed!!! She was totally wet from top to bottom by my saliva; I can do anything to her now without permission. I took only seconds to undress her from top to bottom and that day she looked to me a perfect fish, my lips were going down and down and down and down, until they reach the legs, I didn't know what I was doing. we avoid dresses for some time and started the main mission for almost two hours; I realized it was the newest thing for both of us.

I laid on the bed itself for some minutes; I hugged her very tightly producing some extra love. Sweat was coming out of our bodies; I was surprised if we had played football. I could feel my heartbeat was swift and so was hers.

Baby, why this much sweat is coming out of our body, I don't think we deserve this much sweat for what we did.

Stupid, idiot, don't talk with me, she said weaving her hands in dismay.

What happened, see, I never wanted what happened you can say it an accident, I said.

What?

Yeah?

That is why I refused to come in, my energy is lost. She said

That is why I served you eggs first up, I said and she smacked my hand.

I would never talk you again, *cha chuk mukur* (you are bad).

Ok, my *Ghaashu* I know I am bad, let's maintain our energy once more, I said.

What? I will kick you out. She said.

Oh! Hoo! You mistook it; I mean let's have some fruits like we had eggs to maintain our energy.

Haha, she was forced to laugh a bit, she was ashamed and never looked at me and yeah girls do so.

Let's get up, I said.

Close your eyes, she said.

I half closed my eyes to see through the eye corner getting her dressed.

No… no… no… you stupid, it is not fare you have to close your eyes to full, I am shy… she threw the pillow on my head and laughed.

Hahaha you are shy? Then you must not know what we did some minutes before, I said teasing her.

Close your eyes I have to dress up. She said.

It is okay *Ghaashu* (the light of my eyes) I said keeping my eyes closed now.

I have to go now as you know there is no one in the home.

That means you are inviting me, I said wearing a flash of smile on my face.

Never, No…No… I am sorry you will but only after marriage, she said.

Hahaha ok, let's have some fruits and other things before you could leave, I said.

She wasn't able to walk properly, she tried to mask it up but I had caught it already. I can understand why.

I sliced the mangoes, apples and pineapple, a perfect diet.

Pick up, *Ghaashu*, and consume as much as you can, I said.

She picked a pineapple slice and I snatched it from her mouth.

Jaanu, I have to go now. She said.

No, you have to stay here for lifetime, I said.

Off course I will come for lifetime, we kissed each other once more and I hold her hand to release her at the main gate.

Do keep an eye on your health, bye; I am always with you.

I want a smart gift from you when the MBBS results will come. She said excitedly if I had cracked the examinations.

I cannot accompany her till the main road, might get exposed if I did it is the busiest road of that area.

Nothing changed; my parents came next day afternoon with the news that MBBS results are going to be declared by tomorrow morning.

I was worried I start shivering of threat and that is common.

I wasn't able to sleep whole night since the moment I buried myself into the quilt, I was full of imaginations some bad and some good.

My mother could be seen with her head down and crying while my father was red and thunderstruck, I had cocked my legs on a bed to read a magazine but I was surprised after seeing their reactions, they even don't spoke to me, I stepped forward and placed my right hand on my mother's head to ask for the reason, she looked into my eyes and said, beta *result aa gaya hai, teri slection ni hui hai*…(my son the result had come but you are not selected).

I start crying as loud as I could. I could feel some ones hand over my face and body firmly trying to get me up.

I opened my eyes and saw mom and dad in my bedroom asking me, what happened, what happened, what happened my son.

I hugged my mom strongly and burst into tears; she couldn't hide hers and started to shed tears before me.

Mom, I saw a dreadful dream I don't want to sleep here, please take me to your own room.

My mom run her beautiful hands over my face, wiped my tears and clutched my hand to take me to her own room.

I was unable to sleep after that, dreams were considered as a type of news by some people letting me to avoid elaborating this dream to my parents as I don't want to add salt to the injury.

That morning I woke up very early and prayed to Allah for the successful result, I was 90% sure I couldn't make my name into the list.

My father went to town that morning to get the results from a Block medical officer who had some communicative tools. That was the single person who had lots of information and it was nothing wrong to say him World Wide Web of that area. He was a frank man who loved to visit him for helps; he was more of a social servant than a doctor.

I froze, all of us were bowed in prayers my mom was very emotional during her prayers because she was the lady more aware about the conditions of our home, the strength of our family was ten but the income generator was only one.

I wasn't able to get the result unless my father would say it; there were only few radios and a single black and white television in the entire village, even our whole family didn't know what radio was. The concept of gadgets was years afar from them.

I went to my bedroom praying, my rhythm of prayers was broken due to the continuous clamor coming from our kitchen. I could hear my sisters whistling and shouting of happiness.

Sam brother where are you, Sam bother where are you is the hooting I could here. My face changed, I guess I am selected I rushed down as soon as I entered the kitchen my sisters surrounded me with embraces and lifted me into the air with joy, mom and father brought sweets to share and I was worn garlands of flowers and notes round my neck. My entire family kissed me on my face more than they might have kissed me till yet. I could see everyone's faces shining and blossoming, everyone looked fresh and happy if they were born some hours before.

I was the first doctor now from the entire zone where students hardly think to study medicals after their twelfth grade; a topper of class twelfth medicals was now a doctor. Everybody praised me for what I did, it was again a history created by a boy who was immensely dumped into the love for a fairy, a boy who once had heard that love squashes and destructs lives took it as a challenge and today he was seeing himself changing the equation and setting back to back records only with the help of love and nothing else.

I start imagining what Saba's reaction would be when she will get to hear such wonderful news, but before I could ask her everything I had to bring a gift for her.

Next day I found the list of selectees on a news paper, I could count there were 150 candidates and I was at the forth number. I was sure Saba must have got this news as she hardly missed any news paper to read after she found a writer in her.

It was Friday, still the day on the tip of my tongue.

I bathed and got ready for the Friday prayers; I prayed with my heart out and begged almighty for what he gave both of us to make our life smooth and respect worthy, I prayed for all lovers of the world to get married including us. Before I could put my left foot outside the mosque I saw Saba from her back side going towards the shrine of our village. Our village has one of the famous shrines of Kashmir where people from every corner came to get their desires fulfilled. I was puzzled whether to meet her or not, hundredths of males were coming out of the mosque which forced me to think differently and thought to wait her outside till she shall come out.

I waited outside our village park wherein the banner clearly showed trespassers will be prosecuted but I don't care, every day I would see the park full of children and adults gossiping with the main gate closed, such type of banners have no respect now and are meant opposite to the meaning of the writings over it and trespassers were in thousands without any prosecution. I also chose the medium heighted fence as the easiest way to jump in.

I saw Saba coming out after some minutes passed in waiting.

Oh! My *Jaanu*, my sweetheart, my Sam, my life, congratulations! She didn't mind to jump into the park in the same way I did and hugged me very strongly. My sweet baby I am so proud of you. She holds my hand and wore me a golden ring. I refused but she forced me telling I could never see her face if I don't accept. No one was able to see us under the giant wall at the maximum of its height. I had no gift to give her once again it was still to be purchased.

Tell me how you came here today, I asked.

It had promised to donate.......oh! No. No.... nothing I came here to thank almighty simple, she munched up the sentence in mid way.

What donation you are telling about I asked her simply.

I mean you must need to donate something healthy because you are making rec...... rec..... rec..... Records, she got mixed up.

Don't bother my dear, I am not so fool who is yet to get that you had come here to donate something but I want to know about it. No one exclaims donation is a bad thing that you feel sacred to tell me, I am sure you wouldn't mind to donate your kidney, I said lovingly.

My *Jaanu* (my life) I didn't donated anything, she again avoided to tell.

Kidney, I said.

Hahahaha

Tell

I want kidney.

From me

Oh! Hoo! Why are you talking like this?

Yeah, if you want then I am ready to donate.

I will never accept, she said and promised childishly.

Please say "my life" otherwise I will give you your gift back, I promised.

No... no... no... I will say, please.

Okay go ahead.

It was a golden chain which I had promised to donate after your positive results. She said in a low volume covering her cheeks with her hands if I was going to slap her.

Golden chain? I was shocked.

Yeah, it was the chain which my maternal uncle gifted me after I topped the school in matriculation.

I only managed to notice her face like a figurine. I was perplexed what was she doing, we were not high profile people to donate gold and diamond. It only showed the power of love.

Ghaashu (the light of my eyes) why you donated such a precious gift for me? I think you are not so richest to donate gold and diamonds.

Please don't tell me so, there is not a single treasure to be compared with love, your love meant a lot to me and I can sacrifice my life for you, gold, diamond, silver can be brought from the market but love is such a thing which is tasted only by the luckiest people. A person with lots of treasure without having anybody to love is worthless. True love happens once in generations, I am always ready do anything for you, she was telling and I was getting emotional.

Ghaashu (the light of my life) I will feel proud the day I can do something for you, I simply love you very much.

How much, she said.

I love you…you…you…more than the number of atoms in the world. I haven't any measurement so I compared my love to the number of atoms. I thought it was supreme.

Wow!…I cannot think beyond that, you made my life with this sentence but I am sorry you cannot win today because I love you more than the number of atoms in the world plus one, she said in a jiffy.

Hahahahahaha… cheater, cheater, cheater, *Ghaashu* (the light of my eyes) is a cheater who always adds one to my sentence to defeat me. This cheating will not be considered valuable next time, you have to come with another comparison I warned her with an innocent smile on my face.

No, I will and defeat me if you have guts you looser, she said touching my nose with her forefinger.

I know I can't defeat you, my intelligent fish, I said stroking her cheeks.

Your romance is crossing limits you bad baby, she said while stroking mine strongly.

I have to do it only with my favorite human being on the earth sweetheart, how long you could cover yourself beneath your clothes, I said moving my eyebrows up and down making the sentence as real as stars in the clear sky.

Don't try to be dangerous after marriage otherwise I will punish you, she said.

I will never become dangerous but you must be aware about my power so I can carry-on the baby manufacturing process several times, I said if I had only one job to produce only babies out of her.

That sounds much dangerous; if you would ever try to plan for third baby, I will run out of the room to approach ATAL BIHARI VAJPAYEE complaining him that my husband is *disregarding* the campaign, *"hum do hamare do"*.

Hahahahaha... *Gandi bacchi* (bad baby) it is not an issue; tell me how long you would keep running outside and how long you would stay afar from me?

Forever, my darling Sam, I am sorry I cannot marry you; she acted if she was apologizing.

Wow...why you never joined the film industry if you were a good actress, I smiled.

Don't take it lightly, I am serious, she asked before I could see her smile.

Ok my darling jokes apart, come to my home to pass some precious time once again; I said if I was serious.

No, not even once till our marriage, you don't know how much I suffered last time; she said while shaking her head side by side.

What happened to my life? I said lovingly.

No need to tell everything to you, there are some secrets also.

It is not good to keep any secrets between us, please don't keep secrets and your Sam in the same basket. I said eager to know.

Stupid there are different types of secrets, some can be shared and some not, why are you not understanding my romantic baby.

How to say you I had already understood it only few minutes after we were done, I said laughing.

What? You are so, so shameless, I hate you, quit I don't want to talk with you, she said making low sounds.

Hahahahahhaah...I was lying, I make you fool. Hahahahahahaha.

What hahahahaha…Now you lied I know, you know I wasn't expecting you to be so quixotic. You are extra romantic, I think you utilize your mind only in this stuff, she said smiling again.

I will not try to be enough idealistic because I don't want you to run away from my life. I said grinning.

Hahahahahaah it's not like that you fool, girls do love romance but I think you are some extra romantic, I don't bother about all this, let us to get married to show you what can I do. I expect you not to commit any mistake by counting me less romantic.

We got ourselves deep into the funny and humorous conversation no one cares about the time, oh! Shit, it's very late my sweetheart I need to go otherwise my parents would kill me, I had told them that I will be back after only one hour but it goes past four hours. But please tell me when you are leaving to study doctoral. She was sacred.

Ghaashu (the light of my eyes) don't feel tense. You can say that your friend took you home.

That is what I am thinking about; I will try to convince them. Before I could leave please tell when you are leaving.

You don't bother sweetheart, before I go, I will meet you to take prayers, its twenty days still to go; I said placing my hand on her shoulder.

I want date and day, she said.

I calculated and found my mathematics strong to come with the answer quickly, it 3rd July and the day is Monday.

Oh! Shit how I can meet you that day, she was getting red.

Ghaashu (the light of my eyes) I will leave in the afternoon we can meet in the morning session and even I can accompany you to your college if you want.

No, I don't want myself to come alone after accompanying you in the morning; I need to come back with you without attending the classes.

Okay my sweetheart, if you want we can plan to go for a date that day.

How could it happen, if you had to go to the college that day? She said.

You don't take any pains regarding this I will handle it all.

But make sure our planning is fruitful; I don't want problems to be created for you. She said obeying.

Nothing detrimental will happen, my sweetheart, I said ensuring much confidence.

Its good if so, take care.

I will be waiting that day in the morning at the bus stand. I said.

It is all right my darling, she said before I could give her a flying kiss.

Bye. Love you *Ghaashu* (the light of my eyes), I said.

Bye. Love you too *Jaanu* (my life), she said.

I woke up early in the morning that day and got ready before I told my mother that I was going to meet a friend in Srinagar, she questioned about joining the doctoral but I convinced her some way, it was nothing than a lie only to pull out some handsome cash from her pocket which she did. Going for the first date makes it obligatory to carry handsome cash.

I jovially hurried out of my house and start taking big steps. I reached to the bus stop and she could be seen wearing white dress from top to the bottom, I was in puzzle for the first time to identify her because she looked more of a fairy than my darling fish. Wow!, the only word I managed to say when I reach closer to her, she was scented from top to bottom, and the aroma guaranteed if she had emerged from the heavens just now. Her pink lips had a beautiful slightly dark outline both up and beneath; I desired to keep her lips into my heart for centuries to come. Her eyelashes were much like the first moon bending upsides as sharp as a sword. The kohl made her eyes look dazzling and the brown eyeballs on the purely white ground was simply incredible. Her eyebrows looked like a sharp sword ready to get my heart injured to its maximum. Her curly hair was invisible under the white sari making her forehead to shine like the full moon. Her face would glitter and made me to believe that moon can be visible in the sunlight as well.

Ghaashu (the light of my eyes), you look incredible today, any secret behind it; I said seeing into her eyes.

Yeah, you are the only reason behind it, a person who can sacrifice himself for me, it's much more to earn such love, it would be wrong to demand more from Allah and he has sent you into my life to make it memorable and wonderful. If I am beautiful it's because of you, your love makes me to shine additional after every passing day.

She won the battle already, I thought into the bottom heart. Every time she would give explanation full of love, care, kindness, honesty and integrity which lets only a single option to me, to drop my weapons. I can't be as loving as she is; perhaps I had no art to demonstrate my love by words, I can surely, practically!!! She never used a same word to call me with; she always would change them in order to make her love more loving.

Jigar (my heart) [don't be confused it is another name she came with] let's move to our destiny. I said my mom not to panic if I would be late.

Why?

I said there is a party in our college, she said

Wah! That means you swept the hurdle out of your way, I said with gestures guaranteeing I was pumped up.

I am wiser than you; I keep removing the thorns from our ways, she said if she was my boss.

Where you want to go, I asked her.

I don't know, it depends on you and your cash, she said patting my shoulder.

Meanwhile the bus came and we got in.

I want to marry secretly today, I said.

No, way, I don't want to do such type of activity. You should pray for our marriage to be celebrated according to our culture.

I also want this, my sweetheart, having some chips into my mouth.

You start eating this all, these are potatoes I don't want you to be fatty try to lose your weight instead to increase it before marriage, you meat eater.

I have started eating potatoes now to puncher you at the first night, I said looking into her face from the corner of my eyes.

Quit you stupid, she laughed.

I hate chickens now that is why I started eating potatoes at least half kg per day, I said.

Oh! My GOD, oh! It is better to eat thousands of chickens per day than what you do. She said stroking my hand.

It's my personal way, I said if I am a billionaire.

Ok, I would never comment over it ever, I will never ever say anything when you would get trapped in the biggest hardship of your life by eating these nonsense potatoes, she said.

What type of hardship, I said.

How would my parents accept you when they would see a 300kg man coming for my marriage proposal? Tell, tell. She said in anger.

Hahaha, nice joke, but we would elope.

Girls elope with a cute guy not a bulldozer; she said and soon burst into a laugh.

Hahahahah we laughed as much as we could.

This time you are like a fox and try to be like this. She said.

How you can say I am a fox, I said.

I know *jaanu* (my life) I still remember the farewell day where you ate several pieces of chicken like a fox?

If I am a fox then you are a sick rabbit, I said.

How

Simply, I still remember that day when you were eating the chicken like a bride in front of me, actually I should use sick rabbit instead of bride, and she slapped me.

That doesn't mean I don't love eating chicken but it was you who made me go mad by telling you had a girlfriend. I was thinking what to do if so even the chicken refused to go inside.

I didn't tell that, I pointed out you there by giving the clue that her name starts with *S* and ends with *A*

I don't care; I wanted you to say directly my name, she said while picking some chips from the packet.

I am sorry.

It's okay, I want to thank you for saving a life, she said crushing the chips by her teeth.

Hey! Hey! Don't eat chips it will turn you go fat and what if my parents refused to accept you, I said making fun of her.

I don't want anyone, if there are you by my side, I know you love my heart not my physique, she said and I remained looking at her lips.

That was the biggest lie, I love her heart but her physique was something which made me to love her even more. I took her hand and kissed it, I don't care about the crowd in the bus.

One man from the back seat start shouting, *"are we in a bus or rickshaw can't you drive fast"* targeting the driver.

My heart went in my mouth when he cried out the first part of the sentence but found it at its own place when I heard it further. The man looked very dangerous with 99% his face surrounded by dense and long beard and his neck totally buried into his shoulders.

I could see Saba dropping her head into my lap in terror.

What happened sweetheart, are you okay? I said with my eyes wide open.

I am sacred of this man, he looks like a ghost and you know I have Phasmophobia.

Hahahahahaha don't be sacred he looks very dangerous but I think he is a man of good ethics.

What ethics you are telling about, it needs a giant and hard heart to look into his face, I have not even the courage to see, she said with her face totally buried into my lap.

It is not like that my sweetheart, he is a religious person a good one, said I before someone's hips touched my left shoulder.

I rotated my neck and saw a girl standing in the bus, she was not alone but there were thirties more. It was not a newest thing to think about but it is as old as India itself is, at least I was sure British were not this much selfish than the drivers and conductors, I stood up and asked her to have my seat.

Our society is full of selfishness no one thinks of others even the drivers and conductors are not far behind in the list, they would never get satisfied with all the seats being full but they want overload, and the drivers would never start the vehicle until the number of passengers who are standing go more than those who are seated to feel them if they are vagabonds. And this is called democracy and development, I wished the conductors to be very good managers as how excellently they manage to adjust these many people into the aisle. They don't care about the lives the only thing which matter to them is money. Even helpless and selfish rickshaw drivers observe this and the traffic police acts only like scarecrows on the roads.

Saba fall asleep, and we reached the bus stand.

I woke up Saba the first thing she told after opening her eyes was *"where is that ghost"* making me to laugh once again.

My sweetheart he went out we are only two left in this bus let's move out.

We went out planning where to go; Kashmir is such a place where people remain indifferent while choosing a place to visit. All the places are the trademark of happiness, joy, inner satisfaction and contentment to attract lots of people.

It was impossible to pick out a name when you are indifferent choosing one, Saba came up with different choices including, *Tulip gardens, Gulmarg, Baba Reshi, Pahalgam, Sunmarg, Yousmarg, Tangmarg, Bungus, Kokarnag, Verinag, Achbal, Dechigam, Mughal gardens, Dargah, Dal lake, Walur lake, Uri power project, Eco park, Dr. Sir Muhammad Iqbal Park* and lots more, We were totally indifferent and thanks to my beautiful Kashmir which has made the world go crazy by its beauty and charm, I love my Kashmir, muahhhhhh. I am glad to get birth on this heaven.

It took long time to decide Gulamarg, the land of mighty landscapes, never ending gardens and meadows. We reached there after spending approximately two hours in the Tata Sumo, thanks to Tata Industries to make us to travel fast. The meadows and the landscapes look beautiful and fresh. The existence of different species of birds that would fly only some feet above the ground was something amazing and eye-catching. The white people from different corners of the world could be seen gossiping around and taking pleasure of the horse riding. The gondolas witnessed different races of people to fly over the mighty mountains; the gondolas were at peak of their business as they took off continuously without any delay and the passengers waiting in bulk. Different people were dressed differently it's not so difficult to identify a person from their dress codes. Short skirts, miniskirts and tight fitted jeans received the glimpse of my eyes firstly. Kashmiri people never wear these types of dresses but these dresses are as common as oxygen in the western countries. The landscapes were full of different kinds of things surrounded with; the vehicles looked if ants stood still on the green platform. People could be seen taking photographs giving funny and serious poses in front of the water bodies, fountains and lying on the green carpet. The speedy horses run swiftly here and there with the passengers seem if they are going in the battles like ancient times. The flowers add the beauty, they would move either side by the slow blowing air and the gardeners could be seen pinching out the weeds at the base of the flower plants. Whole of the parks and landscapes looked dazzling and gorgeous in worldwide colors. I was sure I had found worlds each and every color around me without any enmity and selfishness the world looked fresh and calm. Every individual looked very happy with their life having their minds as transparent as glasses. Battles and wars and quarrels and selfishness looked only a rumor on such a beautiful and colorful world, it wouldn't be wrong to say that it seemed if our creator had a direct contact with such smiling faces. Saba was scrutinizing the environment and smiling.

Jaanu (my life) what a masterpiece, she said.

I know my sweetheart; he is the greatest who has made the earth like heavens for us to live in, I said.

See clouds how fast they move, she pointed towards the sky.

I wonder to see clouds moving at such speed. I wasn't a scientist or an astronaut to give her the perfect answer.

We both laid down horizontally on the green carpet and start predicting our future.

Before anything could begin I hold her right arm from wrist and pulled a gift from my pocket, a Titan ladies watch, a gift that she had demanded for the first time.

I joked you that day *Jaanu* (my life) I don't want this. She said.

My sweetheart how innocently and calmly I accepted your gift, it's not gold but at least gifts worth the same no matter how precious they are. I said.

How can you compare a small ring with this Titan watch it is much costly I know the brand. You simply keep it, I promise to demand costly stuff once you will start earning. She said.

I pulled her wrist to get that watch into her shiny arm. It looked splendid on her white fleshy arm, at least you could remember me each and every moment before you could notice the time, I said.

You're true I never remember you any time, I only know I use to remember you only once and that is when my heart beats, she said after keeping her head on my right thigh.

I wasn't such modern to find a reply to such a loving and caring message, you won once more my darling; I simply love you very much.

You have to promise not to give me such precious gifts till our marriage. She said.

Hahahahahah I will try not to give but if it is national emergency then? I said.

Don't talk like this national emergency is when I need blood or organs, she said.

What to do in such case, I said.

I don't know she pricked my thigh and smiled.

Ouch!!!!

Now I expect you not to talk like this, she said coming close to my lips when I was paining.

Ok, my *Ghaashu* I will never, I said.

I liked that, paining and still telling me *Ghaashu,* she said.

See, you don't spend your cash unnecessary, I do want to collect gifts but it's not a proper time, your studies is not so simple now its costly, once you will become a doctor I will start demanding gifts. She said innocently.

That time I would not give you gifts. I said.

Why?

We would be having number of children to feed that is why, I said seeing her through my eye corner.

Number of children, number of children, she lifted her eyebrows and said it twice in surprise.

Yes, number of children, I said.

Only one and that too if I give permission, she said

Oh, hoo hoo, hahaha *tala walah che*, (by GOD?) I said taking her sentence as a joke.

Jokes apart, I want various things from you as gifts, firstly I want a big new home to live in. Smiled!!!

And then

I expect you to get luxury gifts, jewelry, diamond and garments for me without any arguments, understand? I will never wear or eat a local brand, she said with cutest smile on her face.

Sweetheart why are you conversing only about brands when I am ready even to you give you my blood. I said.

I have already told you don't talk like this, I didn't feel good. You are really bad, why are you trying to make my mood off?

I am sorry, let's go back to your brands, I asked.

That is like my sweetheart, she said touching my cheeks with her fingers.

Have a say, or give me a list of things you want. I said.

It's nothing yet, you must know I want to explore new places across the globe and you need to take me whatever place I ask for and as keeping a hobby of gadgetry and clothing I want shopping at least thrice a week and I will never wear any three months old garment. She said seeing deep into my eyes waiting if my response was otherwise.

Wow, wow, its supreme I wanted to have a wife possessing same characters, I don't know how to thank almighty who blessed me with you, having not a bad smile on my face.

Another thing is I want you to cook maximum times, she told but I never got surprised as I knew I have discovered myself a good cook over past few years.

Anything more you want my sweetheart, I asked.

More things to go, I will make out a list and will handle it to you.

Now be attentive and listen about the things I am planning to demand your father, I said.

No, you can only talk about them once my wishes are fulfilled.

You selfish fish, how can you be so egocentric, the fish word again sounded good as she said.

What if some one of us dies before, she asked.

No one among us will die before or after, I said.

Jaanu (my life) I can't see your demise, before I could I would die myself, she said with some emotions.

I want us to die at the same time, embracing each other very tightly which could lead no chance except to get us buried into a same grave in the same cemetery to make it a history. I said if I was begging Allah to do the same with us.

Sometimes, I think about my future and got nervous as how to convince my parents who consider love an affront and offence. She said confusingly.

My sweetheart my condition is also the same, I haven't told you anything about my father, he is very strict, it wouldn't be wrong to call him Hitler-II, I don't know how harsh and hazardous would be his reaction if he would know this. I said.

To be the villagers and that too Indian is the biggest problem, here even urban and high profile people consider love a crime, how could our parents be the exceptions I am so sacred regarding this, she said.

My sweetheart love marriage is very tough job it's as impossible as to see the air, we have a live example in our neighborhood a man hanged her daughter for this reason some four years before.

How terrific, please don't tell me this I will die otherwise, she said while burying her face into her palms.

Our parents are not so malicious at least they can't do such terrible activity, I know. I said.

Each and every parent becomes pitiless and unkind after hearing the word love. Love is the most hated word in Indian civilization. This word has got peak respect in modern and advanced countries, like USA, Britain, and other western countries. She said.

Once we will get married we will switch to western countries to take some pleasure of this word, am I right? I asked.

For what purpose you would go after our marriage, I want to be there right now as I am very upset about our future, she said.

Thank you, now I came to know you don't want to go anywhere after marriage, good girl, I laughed.

I will kill you, I don't mean that, she said.

My sweetheart, have anybody told you about me. I said.

Yeah, my friend *Shaazu* had told me earlier in the friendship days that you could prove a good husband of your wife, but then I didn't know it would be me. She said.

That sounds good, this boyfriend is everything to you, I said.

Sweetheart isn't you my husband, she said innocently.

Yeah, my darling I am you husband under construction and you are my wife under construction, I made her smile.

Then why you never used this word in your previous sentence, she asked.

I am sorry my darling, I will not commit such mistake again, I know you are my cute wife.

Jaanu (my life) my love doesn't allow me to call you my boyfriend nor I want you to say me your girlfriend, because only cowards use these words, at least we are greatest love birds and we need to use some words with a greater impression, value and meaning, boyfriend and girlfriend doesn't get matched with our love.

Love you my wife, as much as the leaves exist on the earth, I smiled.

Wow, new invention, I love you too as much as the distance from earth to sky. She said.

For some time, I thought her sentence was more powerful before I came to know nobody could count the leaves existing on the earth, but her comment as technical hence defeated me once more.

My sweetheart the time is past 1: pm, let's have some food, in the restaurant.

Don't you want me to see your face again and again? It is the biggest treasure I am getting, it satisfies my heart, she said.

My sweetheart I know but we need to get something down our throat so that we could talk with much more energy and zeal. I said.

But don't order any costly food I will not eat if you did, I promise. She said.

What is this you neither want to eat nor accept my little gifts, is this a love? It is not overall, I know you care about me but please don't make these little things to prove a big difference between us, be positive, my sweetheart. I will feel glad by getting a demand for anything from your side.

My life, I told you once you will start earning, I will become the greatest consumer of your earnings and I am warning you never feel gloomy, she said.

Future will talk about it, let's have our lunch first.

She didn't agreed anything to eat costly and forced me to eat the lowest priced dish, it was nothing but rice and fried pulse.

It was time to explore, we captured photos with different poses and also took some snapshots of the beautiful scenery, we had a horse riding and went to lawns and the cold water pools. We even captured the water bodies and the different varieties of plants that we saw for the first time. I was surprised to see *Zaheer* with the horse he was one of the bright student of our class but his face had a little validity, I introduced him with my Saba and he felt very happy. He rode us on his horse and added the flavor of the day. We went to and fro, we had some gardening as well, Saba could be doing childish activities she watered all the trees, plants and beautiful flowers and even start talking with the colored birds chirruping under the hot sun. We consumed some time under the big willow tree, and I can compare my love with the breeze and coolness I got under that shaggy tree, my heart went to have some extra pleasure from the breeze that adds.

The sun could be seen in the middle of the other half of the sky westwards, the water was very cool, and the flowers could be seen shrinking themselves, the birds would fly around the park in search of grains, the clouds came back and spread like a white cotton over our heads but thanks it doesn't last long and the sun was visible once again, the people could be seen going thinner. The reflection of the sunrays through the water body some steps afar from us would discover if a 10000000 volt tube light was lightening the meadows making them look splendid. The cattle and some little pups could be seen entering into the landscape from either side, the pups would crush the chicken boons left over there and the cattle start grazing on the periphery of the park. Animals, humans and birds guzzle the flavor of nature under the never ending skies. That was the picture my beloved Kashmir showed of nature. Its love from every corner, I loved it.

I searched to get a proper timing to kiss her beautiful face but anybody from anywhere kept coming making it not only difficult but impossible as well, time was left very less but again we went round the huge landscapes, at last I was forced to leave without making any romantic scene of the day, it was getting a bit late before we left.

The two hours journey back to our home was extremely emotional, it looked if we were going to get separated forever but it was not so, It was late and It wasn't possible to join the doctorial that day. Before I could say her good bye at the bus stop, she burst into giving me prayers and blessings, it was the last time I was seeing her before we could meet again after some months. She stretched her arms and I got myself in, tight with her chest, it was the goodbye hug and she start weeping, I too couldn't hide the emotional tears, we were going to feel separated without knowing its validity.

Ghaashu (the light of my eyes) I will leave tomorrow morning so please remain at the window pan by exact 7 am.

Ok, my sweetheart I will, and do weave your hand to say good bye. She said and smiled.

Definitely, if the surrounding would be clear. I said and smiled too.

Ok, bye my sweet *Ghaashu*,

See you soon my *Ganda Baccha* (my baby) she said while wiping her eyes.

We looked backwards again and again till we were invisible to each other.

I got myself ready to depart next morning, everyone praised me and kept expectations much supreme than that of before.

Oh! Shit! It is very late, I shouted when seeing the clock had already passed seven.

Papa, when we should leave, I asked.

Your cousin is also going to Srinagar, he met me some minutes earlier, he will be coming at 9am, and we don't have any problem as we have the lift direct to SKIMS.

I was shocked and sad, my face turned to red.

At last we left by 9:10 much late, how could I expect she would be there waiting for my hand to be weaved to say her good bye.

I reached straight to her house and she was seen waiting there, that time I really burst into tears, I don't care my father was also with me, I weaved my hand and so did she, she even gave me a flying kiss.

7

Closeness

SKIMS, was at its peak to produce renowned doctors and I was not an exception. The early results had inspired me to go up for wonders, I know my family financial background and I have to do things accordingly. I didn't enter the college with some other thought except to top the whole batch. To become a skilled, extraordinary and most loved doctor was my only mantra. I start obeying my mantra from the very first day. With time being some professors start calling me their favorite student and that was the thing which lifts and inspired me greatly. Consuming time in unnecessary activities looked not less than dropping poison into the chops of my guardians. I chased my dream unlike everyone in that college. I became a man of my own word and start talking less and doing more. Saba was always there in my heart, it became very tough to live without seeing her or talking her regularly I even don't know anything about such a human who was everything to me. I never looked into only one side of the chapatti, I worked sweat out on my doctoral and love with Saba had become simply an inspiration.

No ideals or role models inspired me as much as her love did I promised with myself to become a changed personality whom over everybody should feel proud. I knew I have to become ten times successful if I have to execute love marriage.

I remember the dates for dates, this day, I saw myself in the library, I could see *Economic times*, a national newspaper I had developed a good habit of reading newspapers, I looked to get it changed and stopped midway after my eyes fall on a news headline *"PM Vajpayee launches mobile services in Jammu and Kashmir."* my mind requested my fast moving heart to concentrate what was written. Vajpayee, fully known as Atal Bihari Vajpayee the then Prime Minster of India is going to launch something new in our state. I don't understand the perfect meaning of the news headline, I could have got but the word Mobile confused me.

My concept got clear it was a communication tool after reading the first paragraph; *"the much awaited mobile telephone services in Jammu and Kashmir were launched today with Prime Minister Vajpayee receiving the first call from state chief minister Mufti Muhammad Sayeed in Srinagar which lasted for ten minutes"* My heart went for a trip after reading the news mostly suited to the couples. Earlier I didn't know what the mobile was but I am clear now. I start guessing how it might look like, like an advanced radio, a television or anything else.

In a few time the mobile services became the talk of the town and soon proved to go super hit move in Jammu and Kashmir. Approximately everyone became crazy to buy this efficient and effective tool and in no time it found its place in the pockets of sixty percent of population. May it be useful for the people working in offices and big industries but it was surely an invention for the people falling in love who could talk nights and days out thus globalizing their hearts and souls till the invention survives itself.

One year later,

I planned to go to home to bring one after insisting my parents, I can bring a piece but it wouldn't be good to purchase it without informing my father.

I went to my home to spend holidays I insisted my parents to bring me a mobile phone. I should have purchased one but I felt it dishonoring my parents without informing them. I could see people talking with each other on phone the more people I could see the more I was getting restless to get a permission to bring one.

My father tried to convince me by giving a one hour long lecture revolving round the same sentence, I can't bring, until your MBBS is over. He attached success and failure at different points respectively only to persuade that it wasn't a good thing for students like me. Even he promised to bring one only after my degree which was five years at distance.

I felt myself uncomfortable to wait for years to get a mobile phone and somewhat I felt it was injustice with the time, five years were not meant for to get hold of such a mini tool. I met Saba the next day she realized if I had no money to bring a cell phone after I disclosed the problem, she picked out some cash from her sack but my love was not so weak to accept it.

Sweetheart, I hadn't loved you for this purpose. I said.

I felt that you haven't sufficient money that is why I am giving you, she asked.

I can purchase not only one but two one for you and one for me. I said in a poetic way.

No, you are a doctor; you need such things but please avoid buying it for me. She said.

Why? I said.

It may be a source to get our relationship known to our parents if it does, don't expect I could love you again, they can do anything to me, she said.

Why are you thinking so negative, you just try and feel the difference, I said.

Because I cannot handle cell phone let the time go as it is going, the day is not for when we could talk everyday at our wish. She said.

Ghaashu I want to talk you each and every day, I said.

My *Jaanu,* I also want to talk with you days and nights but I can't I still don't know how to make a phone run which might cause serious problems for both of us. Once I will find a sufficient time I promise I will ask you to buy one. She explained clearly.

To gift her cell phone forcefully was just like running into a lion's den; I agreed with her decision but purchased one piece for myself only.

Our rendezvous declined with the passage of time but the strength of our love start touching the sky. We would meet after weeks or couple of months, the doctoral was very tough and the challenge to be a great man made it toughest. I hardly had leisure time to waste on my new brought phone; it was Nokia 1100 the common phone then. Initially being addicted to play snake game and would use to learn new things and functions after reading the user guide I went across maximum things hence the utility of that phone went down. Saba, not using any phone was the big reason to keep it locked into my box for next four months to come. Time was little we were growing into adults with same age and same region. I was burst inside to talk with her, every time the presence of the unused phone in the box would make me fidgety. Study was not everything which could make me grow faster and unique, there was a game which I liked most it was none another than cricket, I would spend an hour or two into the cricket ground to keep me physically and mentally fit.

Loving my Saba very much and living my life for her proved very obnoxious to be at a distance from her. Somewhere my studies start getting effected and I got myself very difficult to put control over the emotions, it was acceptable to be her out of my eyes for days but no one want such days to shape in months to make conditions horrible and repulsive.

I forgot my goal for sometime but I knew if I can't do something good she wouldn't be mine even I would feel it cheap not providing a luxurious life to such a person whom I loved the most and whom I had promised to revolve her dreams round the earth. Love marriage in villages happened to be very tough and it was a record that there was not a single such case in our village. The conservatism in the minds of our village people do all talking parents would arrange the marriage of their daughter with an unemployed rather a Prime Minister whom she loves, doctoral stands nowhere, this was the situation of our village and I too felt it was very difficult to insist the people feeding the old mythology into their big unused brains. Everywhere I would see her sketches even the books and everything I could glance upon would saw me her cute pictures. The music I could listen it was not *Alka Yagnic* and *Udit Narayan* the two singing greats singing rather I would feel it was me and my Saba exchanging love and affection for each other into a most loving and romantic manner in accord to the meaning of the songs.

The time was running very bad, I couldn't survive without her like this talking to each other every day was the solution which could chunk impatience out of me.

I selected a date to go home to give her a cell phone not a costly one but at least same as I have. The sun was somewhat pity now, gone beyond the immense clouds but would show its presence occasionally. The city side was dry but cold not as much as mornings and evenings. A person could roam around without putting on many clothes but the chill mornings and evenings forced him to put on anything he would come across making sure the clothes he is wearing isn't any animals' fur.

I was yet to reach my hometown; the atmosphere went changing like typical February days the chill air coming from the busses' casements forced me to pull out the jacket from my bag to be dressed in like a polar bear. To start drizzling heavier and heavier was a matter of time and even its speed and power got increased once I revealed myself out of the bus. The drizzling adds some big raindrops including the cotton like snow pebbles to invade the ground at once, the snow would drop and melt at zero degree temperature, the sky was unseen and the birds start moving to save their nests from getting wet. The animals deposited their tails in between their legs and the chickens would be seen sliding their tail downwards and moving to the safer places.

It was winter, both a friend and a foe for Kashmir; people would get a lot of beauty, the water level of the wells and ponds and other water bodies would increase but on the other hand it would uproot the electric poles making our homes and streets darker for weeks. Once it would get repaired it is destructed over again and again. I rushed into an ambassador car the then most commonly used all-rounder vehicle, people would not mind to carry silage by the same ambassador car meant for carrying the brides and bridegrooms, the car was used for each and every activity, passengers was not the newest thing such cars could carry.

The snow started falling separately now no additional rains; the ground was half an inch covered by whiteness till I reached home. The home appeared the same as it was then, negative changes were visible I could see couple of glasses and the big mirror of my room broken. There was no question to get them repaired; if a stranger would look our houses both from front and backside he will surely say it is a kaput. A house totally faded and the bricks coming out from its posterior part approximately one foot from the pedestal.

Again my father with the same question before I could cross the threshold.

When you have to go back, he said.

Let me to sit first, I don't came for any work, I have to recede in two days, I said with some flesh on my forehead wrinkled to discover some creases.

I had a good time in my house that night my next target was the mobile gallery, I had sufficient cash to bring a SIM card and mobile phone, unlike previous days the routine of getting up late in the morning at home was changed by the strict rules and regulations at the medical college. I rushed out to the market before I could have lunch targeting to be back by 3pm at the bus stop to meet my Saba to give her the phone.

I purchased the same phone in slightly lower price; I felt myself spanking as I left to meet her at the bus stop. I wasn't sure she could meet me but the probability of getting her there was near to one because she hardly misses classes.

I experienced a new Saba at the bus stop after she came out of the vehicle, a tall looking girl maintained from top to bottom with something in her hand. She couldn't expect what she was seeing, she got puzzled to see me but finally we shook hands and start our proceedings.

My sweetheart is it true whatever I am seeing, she asked me.

It is okay if you believe but if not then your love is faded up, I smiled.

Four months without seeing or sharing words with anyone was a nasty epoch, I want to walk off with you somewhere to hug one another extreme tightly so that even the air couldn't pass in between, she said looking deep into my eyes.

No need to go anywhere, you can hug me here, I said.

People around us, she pointed to an old man continuously looking us and smiled.

You don't know how I spent these months, I was about to go mad, I explained.

Is it your heart or a rock inside your ribcage, at least you should have come once or twice to meet me, doesn't you care about me my sweetheart, how can you behave like this, she was getting emotional.

Ghaashu (the light of my eyes) it doesn't mean so, and you must be aware whatever I am doing is nothing but a contribution to make myself a strong candidate available to your parents for you to get ourselves married in a respectable fashion according to the culture and tradition. I said.

Jaanu (my life) it's okay but it doesn't mean you would remain out of my eyes for months like this, she said.

I am sorry, I promise there is no possibility to repeat it again in future, I said, keeping faith over the cell phone which I had to hand her over.

That is like my sweet baby, I don't want to feel myself apart. She said.

Ghaashu (the light of my eyes) you know I am always with you, distances don't impact a relationship negatively rather helps in soaring the love, trust, attraction and affection, it is good to have such times to let you know the value of love. I said.

These are only filmy jokes, it suits to some extend and believe me I cannot resist the ache I use to get by missing you even for a second she expressed more pain by her innocence.

Anything else, I mean interesting, I said letting this chapter away.

What could be more interesting and important apart from us, you and me plus every relation between us is of great magnitude. She said.

I kept the cell phone in secrecy but bequeathed the fruits which I had brought for her. My sweetheart I want to say you one thing before I could leave, I said.

You can, each time anything, you have the right, but before you I want to say you something very beneficial. She said.

Okay have a say about it, I requested and broaden my lips.

If you had time we can meet tomorrow as well, I am going to some relatives at exact 9 am I request you not to make a mess please, otherwise I couldn't meet you. She said.

Okay my sweetheart I will, I wish I could be on time, but you don't bother simply wait me at the old bridge. I will be there on time.

Next morning, the bridge witnessed me to wait her for minimum ten minutes before she could arrive. It wasn't free from danger to talk with your beloved when the big helmeted policemen would gloat you if you were the prey and they were the vultures. India is a country where even beggars are corrupt making sure they wanted to explore an opportunity to seize some cash after deceiving us by thrashing some never made laws. I tweaked Saba to quit from that place to a hotel to have something. She didn't refused that day, had she done I really would have slapped her, we went direct into the hotel, a building to which I was scared of, nobody knows when did you get raided into hotels when you are accompanied by a girl . The corrupted employees in the hotel had a direct contact with the police to inform them if any couple got an entry in the hotel, it was nothing but one of the ways to generate income being the cause of antipathy I had for hotels and restaurants.

Saba nodded too to get into a hotel to have something; she preferred an espresso bar to order coffee.

I focused more on the entrance gate rather on my sweetheart and pulled out the mobile phone from the polythene after passing fine ten minutes there.

What is it? She said.

A small gift, you can call it a weapon which would help us feel more close. I said.

A mobile phone, she said anxiously.

Don't be terrified my sweetheart it isn't a ghost, I said smiling recollecting she had some phobia.

She hauled up the sachet and found the Nokia 1100 mobile phone after opening it.

Haaaaa...... how can I handle it, what if my parents came to know I have a secret phone, it was all she said while blocking her mouth by her fingers.

Don't you have the habit to speak sunny, I said.

You keep this one, I will try to purchase my own, she said.

I know it is cheap, but you need to keep my heart, I said.

It is not what you thought, okay will keep it, even how much time could I survive without your voice going into my ears, she said lovingly.

I got converted into an audience watching Charlie Chaplin performing on the screen. She also laughed after seeing me laughing. The biggest problem is solved I thought inside. I gave a call to her phone to check the electronics of the phone which happened to be satisfactory. The time passed very quickly and we signed off from the espresso bar. There was not a comfortable and secure place to have some gossips at, everyone would gawk us after every foot step if we were their enemies forcing me to think to pluck out their eyes and serve them to the stray dogs. Love never exists in the minds of those people, it was such a place where even men would beat their wives harshly plural times a week, and I had witnessed some of such incidents. We never let any another to know what was running between us. It was very difficult to handle things carefully and roaming in the market was not out of danger. Both of us were sacred if someone from our village could see us together.

I went to a cafe and brought two nut crackers and couple of biscuits; Saba as usual nodded at first up but accepted to suck it. We walked through each and every street and covered almost ten kilometers, new youth somehow smiled at us while nobody had courage to make the older fellows to smile. Our bellies were empty, whole of the energy was consumed the slipping of mobile from Saba's hands into the drain was a perfect example of our condition that time. The time showed one hour past noon, three hours of continuous walking through the slum streets. It was love which wouldn't allow us to sit like professionals to have something good to eat, our age and our body languages proved all the connections we were having. I tried to walk behind Saba to see her from behind but she was enough wise to get the reason of my little steps, she put her hands behind before I saw half a dozen movements of the most fleshy part of her body. I insisted her to have lunch she accepted it after a long argument.

My sweetheart I am late, have to go to the relatives, she could be heard saying this.

You go, I will wait till you will be back, I said.

It may take much time, I am not sure, she said.

You don't bother about that, just call me if you think you could be late, I said.

She agreed and went off.

It had been three hours when she called me for the first time; I didn't concentrate on the content rather in guessing how sexy her voice was. I hadn't thought her voice would be as sexy on phone her voice brought some sexy feelings into my heart. I only responded to her greetings firstly and don't know what she followed, after full five minutes I found my phone fully dumb beneath my ear, I checked it and it showed, last call duration 1:57. After checking the received call I came to know she has hung up sharp 2 minutes and 3 seconds before.

I had no option except to call her again,

Hello... I said.

Yeah!

Where from you had brought such a sexy voice?

So stupid, I could hear her loud laughing sounds.

I didn't understood anything you asked in the first call, I was drowned into the cuteness of you voice, would you please explain what you was saying.

How sweet my darling, I was saying hahahahaha…. I was hahahahaha…..hahahahahahaha oh! You ……..

Hahahahaha….. What happened sweetheart, I couldn't put control over my laugh and same was the condition with her.

How bad you are, I spoke for approximately two minutes and you don't get anything even you said good bye in the last, it's very sweet, and more over is my voice so intense magical and sexy which excites you even in the market? hahahahahahahaha…. Her guffaw was going louder and louder.

Impossible to put control over me when such a cute and innocent laugh I could hear and being it produced by my most loved human being makes it simply matchless.

Gaashu (the light of my eyes) tell what you were telling, I requested.

No… no. I will not, find out if you can, she said, I could hear she was chuckling.

Okay, don't tell, I am going home. I said with a smile which she couldn't see.

No… I will but before I could say, scream once, oh! Help! Help! Help! Saba's sexy voice injured me, help!

Please forgive me, if I do, no one would even declare me mentally fit and the love secret would be exposed.

I was joking sweetheart, yeah! I was saying, I couldn't come today, but I will call you in the night.

Its good, I left home after saying her *"Bye, see you in the night"*.

8

The Electronic Romance

I desperately waited for her call the phone was full of cash and I had a plan to talk her throughout the whole night. It was now the time to say people good morning but she was yet to call. I set my eyes on the phone dozen times a minute. The night gave the impression of a dawn, no sun, no moon and no stars don't wonder where from the light came, the snow emitted light like a never ending tube light. The white coated world showed everything clear by the naked eyes. I had two blankets and two quilts over me but still the chill dominates. I placed the cell phone over my face after calling her thrice without any response; I lay upside down to doze. May be I could feel the vibration on the incoming call, 1100 Nokia's were good to produce a bear wakening vibration.

I woke up, I don't know the time before seeing the mobile…

Oh! Its 5 am …. No phones no missed call.

I checked if I had received one during the sleep, found none.

I again called her and after full thirty four calls I got a missed call, I called back.

Hello…..good morning. Where are you, no phone nothing, what happened sweetheart, are you okay.

My sweet baby, I am fine and sorry not to call you, I think you have got I was uncomfortable.

Yeah, I can understand, I got you may have slept with some elder female.

Hahaha…Yeah, my elder cousin sister to whom I am very sacred and respectful. I liked the way you sad elder female, she said after having some control over her laugh.

Oh! Hoo! I used it to give you a clue of sharing our bed forever after marriage, we both laughed.

Hahaha…you look very much dangerous, seriously. God knows about me after the first night. She said.

Hahahaha…*Ghaashu*, good girls never speak like this.

Just saying dear, I don't know why I think my survival after marriage is followed up by a bulky question mark, she said and I could hear her laughing.

Hey! You just tell you want good morning kisses, you look thirsty, I said with a smile.

No, no, get it out of you head, and even try to be present in the real world.

I am.

Never

Then

In the world of nomads

How

Because they remain naked all the time, she said.

Hahahaha…doesn't you had any other example, I mean some beautiful example like you.

I think you have a doctoral in sexology, she laughed again.

Hahaha…bad baby, I don't have any, but I think I have doctoral in excietmentiology.

Excietmentology? Hahaha she burst into laugh, what is this hahahaha she never wielded control over her laugh.

I am truthful my sweet heart, I said.

No, no, I think, I think, laughing made her to struggle to add it further.

Say? I said.

I know you are a great kisser, I think you have a doctoral in Kissology, she said and I could hear what happened to her after telling this she went mad of laughing.

Hahahahaha…kissology? I roared of laugh, whatttt ….iiisssss…..tttthisss…I put my hand beneath my belly due to pain of laughing.

You don't know, oh hoo how sad then you have must read huggology, she said struggling.

Hahahahah….please don't make me die, hahaha, please get mercy on me now please don't say any more humorous otherwise I will call policeology, hahahahahah…we both got faint of laughing.

It is the super morning ever we have covered whole biology, she said and we laughed again.

Yeah! It is the funniest morning; got me crazy I said wiping my water out of my eyes.

I don't have strength to tell something more, she said.

Where is your cousin sister tonight's sleeping partner, I again laughed.

She woke up a minute before I called you, she said.

She woke up and you got a chance to talk, yeah? I said.

Obviously darling, I was crazy to talk to you after seeing thirty four back to back calls. But I had kept it in the silent mode.

Silent mode… good…That means you learnt things from the user guide.

Hahahaha, yup! consumed some time to get some functions yesterday.

Keep it up, good to hear, but please do visit the phone after some intervals.

I was uncomfortable sweetheart; otherwise I should have called you.

No matter, I can understand. Any plan to come home today.

Precisely, I can't consume days at other places when you are at home.

It feels good, how was the night.

It was irritating, watered my plans completely. I was getting angry.

The winter forces people to sleep close to each other; even I had a small girl sleeping with me. Little babies are like induction heaters, so warm and hence the environment under the quilt gives an odor of summer. But note, I would never let our children to sleep with us.

Hahaha why so?

Because I don't want everybody to know what we use to do once the lights are made dysfunctional. I said wearing a cute smile over my face.

Hahaha… You are right; she could be heard laughing over my micro joke cum reality.

Anything else, I said.

Yeah! I will be coming today and I have to visit the mart to bring something.

I will be waiting at yesterday's place; do call me once you would leave. I said.

I can't meet you darling; my elder brother is accompanying me there.

Okay, do bring something for me as well.

It doesn't seem difficult only but impossible too. You can't try to be over smart in front of him.

After all he is a policemen, they are trained, "You", I was joking I beg you to don't create any problem by trying to bring anything; I don't want you to be caught in any inconvenience.

It depends on the situations; the favorable one can get a gift an unfavorable nothing.

I don't want anything accept you that too full, I could hear someone screaming her name.

It's time to get up, today's sleeping partner is shouting, you just get masked yourself into for further an hour or so, I will catch you in few minutes with some news.

Okay, bye, love you very much my sweetheart.

Bye, hope to call you soon. Love you.

I don't looked outside the glasses, they were foggy and sweated from inside, the room was little darker. I waited for several minutes before my mobile could produce incoming call ring.

Trin... Trn... Trin... Trin... Trin... Trin... Trin... the black and white screen flashed "MY LIFE CALLING."

HELLO...

Oh! Hoo! Ho! Everything is totally dumped under the snow, its two feet approximately and chill air is blowing around. I froze; want to expand the night by three hours more. Minimum!

Haha...even I want the same with you besides me, I said.

You can't do anything, oh! Ok, bye she is screaming my name once again, bye.

See you soon....love you with lots of kisses on your entire body.

Bye...and I hung up.

Her phone made me crazy to get up to see what had happened outside, Oh! My legs obscure, approximately two feet and still going on. Kashmir got dressed white here and there. I hardly found any shrubs and little plants as they were drowned into the snow, the white semisolid water was falling like cotton from the heavens, the roads, the stones and the fence around our home had submerged. No transport would be there for several weeks I was sure. The voice wouldn't go very far and thanks no mud will be there. Children would love to hum again and again after stepping on the smooth powdered snow. Whole winter is made for children, they dominates these snowy months what adults could do in summers. There was hardly anything to do for me that day except watching people marching towards the town side. Everyone looks ten times fleshier then they actually are with hardly any neck and hardly any bones. People look if they are blowing gases into the air when they would talk or breathe; their nostrils seem if it is a double steamed pressure cooker blowing out the steam with giant force. I came in and slept once again.

The 1100 Nokia phone showed it is 12 noon means some extra rest.

I felt the vibration, it was none another, my darling Saba. Hello…

I could hear her hyperventilating, are you okay, where you are.

Marching home, no vehicle to travel by, I don't know where actually I am, the snow made every place to look same, I am sacred enough, no people is seen around except some big bruisers' six or eight in number with confused hair and their body covered with much fat clothes, I don't know what to do except to walk fast.

Oh! Fuck…oh! How could you mess up if you are aware of everything? My face changed red and eyes came out.

You know I don't want to consume days at some other place when you are at home.

Hell to this all, I already start running to catch her. I start breathing heavily.

Sweetheart… just be hearing me and never move your phone from your ears I am coming. I start taking big steps.

It is okay, I will. She was shivering.

Hello…hello…Hello…

Fuck……………the battery is gone; I couldn't hear it warning earlier.

I run with all my might, Kashmir, a place where everything is possible and everything is impossible as well. One couldn't leave young girls stray as the rascals had a very bad record since past years.

Almighty please save her, almighty please save her, almighty please save her, the mantra I could repeat every time. Almost four or five kilometers and still going, my legs froze and I got tired. The road wasn't clear, dumped with snow; I would stumble and fell down numberless till I could see her familiarizing herself to them, I guessed.

Ghaashuuuuuuu (the light of my eyes) I am coming, I produced an ear-splitting volume.

She rotated her neck and starts running towards me before one of the bulldogs clung her hand and grabbed her back.

That scene almost made me mad; nothing came out of my throat till I reached there and hugged her in front of the bastards.

Bastard… What are you doing, one of the scalawag said in a harsh tone.

I said, Sir! she is my neighbor whose father is an army colonel, recently posted in Srinagar. It was the biggest lie I had told yet. There was no other option to get them sacred because the troops had a decent dominance over Kashmir youth since couple of decades.

Yeah! Yeah! That was the only reason we were introducing her, other one with big moustaches said.

Sir, I a doctor, and she is my bride. Our marriage is fixed on 26th next month, let's go.

It's okay. You just show your identity.

I pulled out the college identity card followed by the voter ID. I knew how could these illiterates know what was written.

Yeah it's good, you just go, and we need to talk to her about her father.

He is an army colonel, I don't think you would have any link with him, please let us to move from here.

Don't try to be over smart, we need to approach him, as we also want to get selected in Indian army. One of the bullshit screamed, I knew they spoke lie.

Sir, I can't leave from here, we have to do some shopping for our marriage.

What the fuck you are telling, who the hell said you that there is a bit link between marriages and winters.

I am saying our marriage is still one and half month afar, there will be no winter that time, I tried to clear every point.

We don't care, you just quit from here otherwise we can be harsh.

The surrounding was foggy and we could hardly see anything even meters away from us, everything was silent and troublesome. The snow dust starts falling from the twigs. Apart from humans animals were also invisible. There was no body to help us as my situation was getting worse. There body language was fearsome, I gestured Saba to leave from there so that they may become week but she nodded, telling how she could leave without me.

I noticed an army snow crusher eradicating the snow to get the roads functional. The road was getting little comfortable for vehicles. The vagabonds would come with different reasons to make me quit from there but how can I, when my heart and my life is clinched by them. Meanwhile an Ambassador car was seen coming with red giant blub twinkling on the top two wheels of which were surrounded by the metallic chains to avoid slither and slips. We're gone my heart murmurs inside. Saba came closer to my chest but the rascals look sacred.

The Ambassador car stopped besides us to make me breathe faster thinking we would be carried to some secret place and killed.

Sam… what are you doing here, there is no vehicle to travel by come with us, a voice came from the car.

I couldn't believe it over. Before I identified it was my father's fast friend a police officer.

Yes sir, I was waiting for one to come but it didn't, hiding the main reason to be there from past one hour.

I hold Saba's hand and let her go in first.

Saba couldn't believe we can move now, I gawped at them and went into the car.

After full one hour, we dropped Saba at her home; I kept my eyes fixed at her till she went into her house.

I got out of the car at my home thanking him for the lift, I did ask him to come and have something which he responded with thanks only.

There was still no light, but one of our neighbors had a big generator, I put my phone on charging and start thinking what, if that ambassador car wouldn't have arrived? There was anything possible but before going through the incident anymore I opted to call Saba.

Trin…trin…trin…trin…trin…trin… no answer.

Trin…trin…trin…trin…trin…trin…no answer.

Trin…trin…trin…trin…trin…trin…no answer.

Trin trin trin trin………..hello…

Yeah, where were you.

Oh! I was in the kitchen with my mother, I was no options left except to avoid besides feeling the vibration.

It's okay!! And it is good not to take risks, but tell me what the mess you made, are you mad?

What happened?

How could you leave for your home without anybody to accompany, you are mature girl and doing so is never out of danger.

My brother called my cousin sister to let me come that he will be waiting in the market, she said.

Fuck your brother who even doesn't know the situation besides being a policeman, hell to him. I was burning inside.

How many times should I tell you that females are the most targeted gender not only here but in each and every corner of the world? Don't you know I was about to die? I beg you to please be careful henceforth; please don't make me to go mad, I will give you lessons what to and what not to do.

Actually I didn't want to spend days at some other places when you are at home, she said.

I know my dear but life comes first then is love, you can only love me when you would be alive, I said.

My sweetheart I am sorry.

I hate you for not being careful to yourself; I think you would kill me by doing all these things.

Now see I am touching your feet, please pardon me, please, *Jaanu* (my life).

Oh! What are you saying my dear? I know you did it for me; I simply want you not to jump in love so deep that you may forget to care yourself.

Are you sad, my *Jaanu*, she said.

Not sad, but I am shivering and shocked.

Forgive me now, please, she said very emotionally begging me.

It is all right now, I said.

No you are not true, she said.

Really my dear, by you, I said.

Then kiss me ten times, she said.

Oh! Ho, ok, ok, muahh, muah, muah, muah, muah, muah, muah, muah, muah, muah, happy?

Extremely happy, love you very much for such a care you showed today.

How stupid.

Oh! Mom is calling me, hope to catch you in the night, till then take best care of yourself, she said dumping quickly.

Don't be smart my little innocent and fool sweetheart, I said followed by some more electronic kisses she was wittier than me she kissed me dozens of times when I had hardly completed six or seven.

Jaanu (my life)... See, just give me a missed call or two, I will call you once I will get I am comfortable, he said with immense love.

You do your work and please avoid risks, hope to see you in the night. I said.

We had a routine to kiss one another very sexually before we could hang up. But there was a difference between mine and her kisses, she would kiss quiet and short while mine would be horny with long hums if I was doing it all practically and would suck the keypad with curiosity till making it sopping.

Time was going ahead very fast in the chill snowy winter. The snow was on fire, no signs to stop; it had already reached to kiss the window panes. I called her and after sharp ten minutes I got her call back.

I disconnected her call and called back.

As usual we greeted one another being the only formal we could do during nights and I hope you would never question what happened next.

How are you my sweetheart, I said vigorously.

Same as you are.

I am good.

I am also good.

If I say I am not good then?

I will not be good more even, she laughed.

Something new, I said.

Jaanu why you never attend my call, she asked an open question.

Just leave it, it's simple, I said.

I questioned it means you have to answer, understand, she approached with a fake anger.

See, your father is not what my father is that is why, I gave a typical answer.

Means

I mean, your father has wages and my father has income.

Means

I know you got it.

Oh! Ho! Don't think such deep, I know my father is a tailor but our monthly income is two times more than yours, she had some confidence.

How

Only your father is earning in your family and in our family it is three, my father and two brothers.

Don't count brothers; they have to feed their wives and children.

It is but you do attend my call, maybe it is an emergency at some time, then?

Ok, I will but for some minutes that too now and then.

I had never even dreamt about such a husband with such incredible traits and love.

With Almighty's blessings I would prove to be even caring. I said.

That is why I love you, she said.

That is why I kiss you, we both laughed.

We have incredible days I don't think there is any other as caring, loving, funny, gentle and above all romantic like you. Sometimes I think about our married life, how prosperous and loving those days would be I can't imagine how happy I would be with you. Sometimes I wonder how lucky I am to get you to make my life to blossom. I love you.

Even I think I am the luckiest who have such a human in my heart to make it survive for centuries; there is no one as beautiful as you. You are my heartbeat.

My life has become quiet impossible without you we are incomplete without each other my sweetheart you are the sun and I am its brightness, you are the snow and I am its whiteness, you are the flower and I am its color, you are the heaven and I am its aroma, you are the moon and I am its beauty, you are the ground and I am its soil, you are the ocean and I am its water, you are my heart and I am your blood, you are mine and I am simply yours. I love you now and always, she said lovingly.

My *Ghaashu,* you made my life with this beautiful message, I don't know how and what I am but I know whatever I am I am for you, I said when I had no words to say for her.

It's very good to gather such message from you in such a creeping cold, she said.

The snow will not stop as it seemed, it looks very dangerous. I said, trying if she had same perceptions regarding the unstoppable snow balls.

Oh! Yeah! It is turning very dangerous, I even think that the buildings are going to be knocked down, and it bears a chilly environment making everybody to remain chipped with the room heaters and the earthen pots and hearth.

My sweetheart I am masked under couple of quilts and blankets. I said.

I made myself obscure under the quilt. The chill grows up strongly and secondly I don't want my voice to go out for a walk to get me exposed, I am dead if it did. She muttered under the quilt as her voice became already little faded.

Your voice is little uncomfortable, I said.

It would be, don't you know I have even my head buried into the quilt.

Just be normal, why are you making it difficult.

Nope, I am afraid, they would set me fire if they would ever come to know about this, it's a coincidence that my sister is not here letting me have some gossips with you this night, otherwise it wasn't possible, she said.

It's all right, that means we aren't able to talk like this daily?

It seems impossible to talk every night but we can make it to call for a good time during days.

Hope so but I beg you not to create any problem for you, try to call me only when you realize you are comfortable no matter if it would last for weeks your safety is everything, if you are safe and happy a single day is equal to thousand years for me. Don't create a doubt into the minds of your parents, obey them like you does and try to be as normal as you were before.

It's all right sweetheart. I practice this only.

You are the daily newspaper reader, come to the point of womanhood.

What womanhood.

I mean come to the blinder you did today, I said.

Leave it now, please, I had already said sorry for that, she said.

No, I want to give you some lessons, I said.

Wow! That is very good, love you.

See, you are born here and are aware about everything happening here and above all you are a daily newspaper reader and more over you are a female.

Yeah my sweetheart

You know everything about the women abuse in our state and the rape victims seeking justice from the government since years, no doubt the world is full of humans but it wouldn't be wrong to say it lacks humanity. It's very difficult for a woman to spend her life smoothly. But our state is the unique example where both men and women are sexually assaulted on the name of our freedom. The troops and the bastards don't even get mercy on the minor faces. My sweetheart what was the fault of the innocent fifty three females including girls below ten of Kunan Poshpora when they were gang raped by the Soldiers of the 4th Rajputana Rifles of Indian army on 23rd February in our district Kupwara. Not this there are various other cases which almost take our life away. There are different kinds of people living our surroundings, some are good and some are bad. Some are our friends and some are foes. The goons never bother about the lives of females, I know you are quiet frank with each and everyone but I would declare it somewhat wrong, being frank and making different friends must need a boundary but your innocence and simplicity has dropped you beyond that limit. You must remember you are a female who live in Kashmir. I request you to bring some aggression into you and be a lady of your own words. Never try to spend more time in gossiping with the male friends in your college and never try to board a vehicle alone. Do keep your chest totally masked while boarding into a bus and please don't remain roaming in the market alone during college and never go to your fields alone remember, you must know the percentage of women harassment and malice is soaring everywhere in the globe, I hope you trust and obey me.

Loved!! I am being cared this much, love you my sweetheart. I could feel she was little emotional.

It's my right; no treasure of the world could make me as much happier as a flash of your smile. You are my princess, made for each other.

I am speechless, today you are the winner and I am the looser.

Not like that, I can do express my love not only practically but by every way I would get a chance through. Love is such a thing which diminishes and is faded up when not executed by hearts, when it is, it can break all the records. A love is not love when you lack care for each other; it's only an affair then.

I am again saying that I am the luckiest girl who is being loved by the most loving human being so lovingly, I love the love you love me.

You can't be more loving than me today; I have the guts to defeat you in every possible ways.

Don't be so over confident, just recollect the previous days, I never allowed you to overtake me, remember, remember, she said taking a long breathe.

If you want to achieve something in the future you need to forget the past then, I don't mean I forgot you loved me but I simply forgot how many times you had won. I said and smiled.

Hahahahaha… absolutely right, even I don't remember how many times I had defeated you.

The number is numberless; my tone goes low, very low.

Don't make your tone low; today be attentive, going to tell you your do's and don'ts of after marriage.

You have already spoken to the greatest; I can hope I could be a very loving and obedient husband.

Why not!! Have you any doubt? If it does, get it removed, drained away yeah! You have to run according me after our marriage, I will make rules for you; her voice turned to be very effective.

Ghaashu, So hard, na na na, I don't like it I am shivering my sweetheart to what things I could be made aware about. If there is any demand let me to know to get prepared for it. I said with my ears quiet attentive.

Don't like demands, for me, the biggest demand is you, I want to spend an uncomplicated life and my desire is to keep your parents as happy as they want to be.

Girls always go saying these many similar things before marriage and once it's done the equation changes.

What do you mean? She said.

You hate your in-laws and husband even, I said.

Shut up, she sacred me with the loud shout.

Let's see, I said.

I am not of such character, I have a dream to be an example; I want to be most missed daughter-in-law, wife, mother and a friend.

So you want to say, you have a dream not to be harsh and wicked to your in-laws?

Yeah?

I also have a dream you may achieve your dream, followed by a giant laugh by both of us.

How bad you are, I can't imagine. She said if I was always bad.

Just avoid imagining, I know you have a low range imagination. Shut up and go away from there. Unfortunately I couldn't keep this joking live for minutes even to let her feel I was serious, shit! I burst into a mountainous laugh.

That's what I wanted, *Ganda baccha* (bad baby) I knew you have got new ways of teasing, it's also one of the big reason to love you this much. Everything you does, you are gaining more love from me, how can I live without you, you simply won my heart by doing everything and as expected I can't hate what you could perform as it would be always declared loving and caring.

Oh! My sweetheart, you spoke beautifully but it would have been more delightful if you would have used joking instead of teasing.

No, never, you went teasing me and that is it, I know I am innocent to get teased easily.

Yeah my darling, there couldn't be another human as simple, loving and as innocent as you, these are the major pillars behind my supreme love.

Don't talk this much high; you are giving me more what I actually deserve.

Its truth which I liked, more over you doesn't want me spending money that is the biggest thing I liked in you.

Hahahahahaha, hey! You! Don't think I will never change my attitude with regard to that; I can't do it this time because you are a student.

So when are you going to change your attitude, I said.

Not now but definitely after you will start earning I will make very precious and sky touching demands which you have to fulfill by crook or by crook.

I will love to get them fulfilled provided if they are into the area of my pocket, I said.

I don't care, it is your problem, I will demand for luxurious items.

Like what? I said.

You just take a copy and pen to get it penned down otherwise you will forget it, she said if she was making an order to a supplier.

You naughty, ok I did. I really took a pen and copy to write it down, these were the words of my life how I could avoid obeying them.

First of all I want a diamond ring on engagement. Pure diamond, she stressed over the words to scare me.

Wow, not enough.

Listen...Want a four wheeler as a gift on marriage ceremony.

I will think about it, by the way it's you who should give me car as a gift. By the way this is what I have to demand, take it as a dowry.

We cannot afford nor will I allow my father to gift you, listen it clearly, she had a gentle laugh.

I am kidding, my *Jaanu*, there can't be a biggest treasure for me above you. Anything more, I asked.

Why not, loads of things to go, I think I have told you it earlier, hope you know.

Yeah! I know. I am sure everything is done, is it?

Not now, I want to explore minimum two places in a month and a visit to abroad once in a year.

Uff uff.... *Ghaashu* (the light of my eyes)... I am extremely sorry I forgot to tell you that I am gay, sorry I can't marry you, I said quickly.

Hahahahaha.....you Charlie Chaplin, hahahahahhaha, oh! I am not able to stop laughing; I could hear her giant laughing voices. I also burst into a big laughter to accompany her.

Mr. Charlie Chaplin never spoke; you even can't compare me with Rowan Ankitson the man starring in Mr. Bean comedy show who normally opens his mouth when he does he makes everyone laugh twice than what they could close mouthed. I said.

The thing my mind goes to sail around is thinking about a purring cat when I use to hear him; he has a purring voice, she said.

I know I only use to laugh and do nothing while watching the shows. I said.

Gem of a person, but you please don't try to copy him otherwise I would die of laughing. There is lot to do. She said.

I didn't understood what she meant by telling "*there is lot to do*" for me I thought she had a hunger to produce Writers, doctors, managers and engineers way early. It was possible thanks she was 18 plus.

For me, you and only you is my life. That is it. Without whom my life is worthless, she geared up to become little emotional while telling these words.

Are you emotional? I asked.

There are always tears in my eyes thinking you are by my side forever as I feel myself lucky, enough lucky to be with such a person who loves me beyond expectations.

I myself believe I don't love you as much as you love me.

This is what our strength is, she said.

Anything special I have to do after marriage? I asked with a hope to get other humorous things to hear.

What sort of question is this, obviously, you need to prepare bed tea for both of us every day.

Me? I said shocking.

It's nothing much… you have to do lots more.

What?

Not any difficult task, simply you have to cook for three days a week and so will I.

Oh!! *Maine khudaya* (oh my GOD) cruel lady, I put down my phone from the ears but lifted it up to them after few seconds.

Any doubt or any change you want, she asked.

Who will cook for the seventh day? I asked.

Hahahaah I have already kept that day to visit the restaurants.

But there aren't enough good restaurants in our village, I said.

Isn't there anyone in Kashmir, she said.

Yeah, loads of restaurants, I came up with a quick answer.

So why do you have pains, she said.

Oh! I got, for her distances aren't the issues, she can even fly to America to have non-veg. I thought inside.

Now you have to think whether you have chosen an innocent wife or a wicked one, she said.

Being the apple of my eye how could you be wicked, this word never suits with you; I brought my lips closer to the phone as the network went little slow.

I checked the watch which showed me, 2:37 am when the second hand was kissing ten. I never felt the chill till yet.

Jaanu (my life)… I am feeling cold, she said.

Me too and do you know how it's cured, I asked.

Yeah! Simple by room heaters, blankets and traditional Kashmiri Kangiris (earthen pots), she said.

Not among the romantic answers, I said.

Oooo, you want that….stupidddd…….

What? I said. I wanted her to inaugurate some romance.

Nothing, she said.

Please.

No way.

Ghaashu (the light of my eyes), please come to me to make me warm, I actually mean sleeping.

Niear latav ho (go away) she used a typical Kashmiri joke and produced a cute voice. She composed it very beautifully, I requested her to say it again and again.

I really want to dive into your bedding this time, I said energetically.

Yeah, you can after promising you will not get naughty or out of control, she said as her voice was pleasing.

That is what I want and getting warmth is merely an excuse, I said jumping to the main point.

What do you want to do, she said and it looked she got activated.

Nothing except to explore all your body parts with zeal, I answered.

After that, she said.

What you actually want? I tried to know if she also had some hunger.

I want to support you quietly and allow you to do whatever you want, her voice start coming with different breakups.

I want kiss you till morning, I said.

Only kiss... enough? She answered short with some excitement desiring for something.

A lot to do once you compromise; it is merely a warm up yet. I said ensuring for high class romance.

I want to hold you into my arms for longer times just to practice everything with you, she said and her voice was already dead.

Come to me please, I said if she was with me at the first night eve.

Do ensure you are not obeying the limits; she was struggling to add each word.

Come to me *Ghaashu* (the light of my eyes), I said with a great zest after some saliva slipped out on the pillow.

Jaanu (my life) I am into your bedding available to cross the limits.

This sentence forced my eyes to get closed I went deep into the quilt preparing myself to share something romantic in a romantic fashion.

Jaanu (my life) come closer to me and give me a tight hug, her words were shivering.

Already very close to you baby, I am feeling the stars into my lap I said feeling on the seventh sky.

Jaanu (my life) kiss me, oh! Kiss me please. She was dying.

Give me your lips; I want to explore everything tonight, ah…ah…ah…my sweetheart come closer.

Jaanu (my life) hurry and hug me; it's all a different feeling to see it looks if the stars are summing to hug me when you are there close to my heart. I could feel she was sniffling of cold to which hugging her was the only cure.

My phone was going wet I was damn sure, she would not agree with seven or eight kisses, for her even hundreds seems less, I would die of kissing if she may say about kissing her thousand times, she was at the peak of excitement. I became immobile waiting and praying for the demand to be in less numbers which off course was an inflexible desire.

Haven't you got blessed with boyish feelings, she said proving I was delaying. But I myself didn't know how and where I was, the bedding was almost shattered.

Ok, sweetie how many kisses to give you, I asked, 1 or 2 or 3 or more? The excitement let me to ask anything.

Ah …. Ah……1, 2, 3, 4, 5, no, no, no, no… ah………. ah……ah……. Ok only fifteen kilos. Fewer amount today, she said if she was about to sleep forever.

Fifteen kilo kisses? I didn't thought much about what she asked me to do rather I jumped up to do the work for both of us. Get up Sam and turn the keypad of you mobile into a dam, I thought into inner. Where from to get fifteen kilo kisses, I don't know nor had I given her kisses in the said unit but yes it was all about to suck my phones keypad to produce sexy sounds for at least fifteen plus minutes like I was heated up.

I went on to my job like an obedient husband. I went on to get fifteen kilo kisses for her, though it was not available on some shop, it was an intangible thing that could only be heard and felt, so I prepared myself to obey what she verbalize.

I started and soon got accelerated without killing much time.

As I went on and on and on and on and she gave the impression like she was gone and gone and gone, I would bite the keypad, her sounds does nothing except to drop me on the peak of romance where from it was very difficult to get down without getting some reward, I got wild and dangerous after each second, I started roaring of excitement and my trousers were almost to burst beneath my belly, you cannot count her out of race, she was racing her race with support of cries and purring all the way, what else was special were her sounds which made me even crazier and we both lost control, I don't know what we were doing but whatever it was, it was of great pleasure, doing it while hearing her sexy and innocent sounds adds the sex center to go way beyond. I produced great appetite to do it thousand times henceforth. Time was the thing we both forgot, we were busy in the doings and certainly we cannot put it to an end easily, sex is time consuming that was what we were doing. She was crying of excitement and after time I felt loose and relaxed but she would kill me I would stop kissing her, I came back to consciousness and found my phone if soaked in a tin of gum, so slippery and watery. I quickly glanced to the phone but remained producing kissing sounds by summing up my lips together because she would murder me if I tried to become hurdle in her project. Oh!...fifteen minutes gone, yeah, I knew her demand wasn't yet fulfilled, she was roaring of excitement herself, for her the demand would be finished once she is done, I was sure, praying she may get done as quickly as possible.

At last I summed up some courage and told her, Sweetie, get pity on my phone now at least, it's too wet to suck it any more, it wouldn't work anymore if I wouldn't stop it now that is for sure. If so, whom will you talk then after? I requested naively.

One more minute, I couldn't listen it properly but the sentence was the same, I guessed as she whispered in a crazy and fanatical tone, I was enough wise to presume her excitement was a guest for some minutes or even seconds, her voice went into my heart once more she was effected and looked at the peak of excitement reflected in her crazy voice. Her voice was enough killing to left some ambition to do it practically once more what was an oral chore tedious task. I could hear the purring and low sounds she was saying good bye; it was an on the spot an authentic proof that she went relaxed and how can't one when he would be hearing such sounds if we were practicing practical practically.

The one minute was yet to get completed, when she murmured, my sweetie, stop and thank you. Love you so, so much, lots of kisses on your entire body, I really want to be with you but hell to our single story house where all got slept jam-packed never allowing to happen something between us again, everything could have been possible if we have had a bigger one, she told in a susceptible mode.

I got why she thanked me in the above lines, you all know as well, nothing to explain. I kissed her for the last time and requested her to sleep till late morning, the clock stuck 4 am.

Ghaashu (the light of my eyes) bye, love you very much, always with you now and forever, I said.

Bye, muahhhhh…muahhhhhh…muahhhhhhh…she kissed me three times more before she could hung up to sleep, it has been five minutes beyond four.

We both went to sleep at last, the night was full of electronics, yeah, and you wouldn't have been unable to see us doing all this before. Thanks to Alexander gram bell.

I didn't know anything about the world even nothing of me till the deafening scream produced by my mom forced my eyes to get opened.

Doctors are not meant to sleep till noon, and you know you have to left for your college in the evening, get ready. She finished her sentence with a lot of stress on the last word…*ready*.

As usual I checked if the time it was kissing noon, *aye maine khudaya* (oh my GOD) I cried out Allah's name after my watch showed it was sharp 10: 04 am, not a time to get up. All that was to do was to jump out to take a bath with typical winter hot water. I got a dirty look from a neighbor who made his steps direct to our kitchen where I was having breakfast, and he may have thought that wasn't any time for a future doctor to get up and who is too mature to bear children. Obviously I can't explain the reason. Thanks my father was not in the home that day otherwise my condition would have been worse.

Niseee… don't feel confused it's the name by which my parents do call me, come on and get prepared for college; your father will be waiting you in the market, mom gave a good yelling.

Matter of few minutes to get ready, I did wait if Saba was calling me, no calls since we hung up for the last time neither did me because she may be busy.

It's from me go and do call once you reach your college; she put some two hundred rupees into my hand and advised to leave as early as you could followed by thousands of prayers.

I cannot leave without calling Saba or without seeing her at least once I was still thinking about it when my phone rang, the screen displayed, MY LIFE CALLING, It was Saba.

I was sure I will get a little late and before my father could find my cell phone in waiting I activated switch off divert and went on to call Saba, for me it was more important to listen her beautiful words before making it towards the college otherwise I can't dare to think to leave my home.

Jaanu (my life) meri umar lag jaye aapko (may my age be added to yours)… where are you, I was missing you very much, muahhh muahh muahhhhh, my heart isn't satisfied yet… muahhhh muahh muahhh muahhhhh…………. She gave me lots of kisses.

Ghaashu (the light of my eyes) I was waiting for your call only, I am about to leave for college. And how is everyone at your home? I said.

There was some problem, she said emotionally.

What happened, my heart went into my mouth.

Grand… grandmot…grandmother…………she couldn't complete her sentence easily.

Please tell *Ghaashu*, what happened, I said before running my hand through my hairs, I got tensed and had already set steps for my college. I changed into a statuette.

Grandmother fell down in the bathroom today morning; still unconscious even the doctors diagnosed only few hours of life in her kismet. She could be heard sobbing.

Oh! My God, I am sorry, I found myself jammed as words refused to come out my throat, let's pray for her health, the only sentence I could manage to ask at last.

I am very attached to her, she had even promised to get me married with you, at least she was there to insist others to get done what I wanted, what if she will sleep forever. Her sobbing changed to bawl.

Ghaaashu (the light of my eyes) what are you doing, nothing will happen to her, she will be fine soon, I tried to console her.

I can understand she had spent her life but her survival till my marriage was the biggest fortune for me as no one had the courage to outdo or brush out her sayings that was what had made me extreme sure we will get married. She described helplessly and I too start losing control over my emotions.

My life, everyone has to go and taste the death, this cup of tea is for everyone, its beyond our control but the thing we can do is try and pray, nothing else, some went before us and some has to come after. All the humans and all the living organisms are sent here only to prepare themselves for the certain death, we all hope her virtues to be enough strongest that will fly her to the heaven core. Anyway I summed up these lines to soothe her.

I don't know why my mind got buried into nasty thoughts and grubby pictures, my life and my everything please hold me into your arms I am seeing our future getting filled with tears, thorns and pains.

Ghaashu (the light of my eyes) I will not let anything appalling to happen, how can you cry this much when your *Jaanu* is with you, I am enough strong to face any hardships, please stop crying, I couldn't bear anymore tears dropping from your eyes.

Our creator is with us, hopeful, he will never do anything wrong, she expressed enough confidence in him, I could listen a lot of clamor coming from her home, everyone was weeping and shouting.

All we have to pray; hopefully everything would be fine and please take care of yourself. I said. *Jaanu* (my life) you are getting late to your college, please move otherwise you would get late; I will be waiting on the staircase for the "Goodbye".

Ok, my life, take care, see you soon. I hung up, no kisses that time.

I boarded into the vehicle thinking all about our future and fuss, I put my head out of the vehicle and could see Saba standing there in dismay gesturing Goodbye and I weaved both of my hands.

I was enough late, it wasn't a time to leave when your journey is more than hundred plus kilometers, my father is waiting me in the market and I cannot omit to count his scold. Precisely he did but allowed me to go.

I reached college through the smooth journey, I did call Saba, I tried various times and she didn't respond letting me turn other option, to call my father.

The movement I was done Saba called me, I cut the phone as usual and dialed her number.

Tri....hello! *Jaanuuuu*, she received the call in a second it felt like she strangulated the phone. She looked happy now.

Yeah! My sweetheart, is everything okay, how is grandmother, I asked.

I was in the middle of the family, grandmother is serious, and I think her pack is over now. She mentioned in the childish tone.

Hahahaha Oh! No, you look okay now. Your grandmother is breathing her last and you are relating it with an internet pack, for a second I don't know whether to laugh or to maintain a mood, but I burst into some more laugh to feel her better.

Jaanu are you okay? And when did you reach your college? Just now, I said.

That's good, you had anything?

Yeah! A cup of coffee and a packet of crackers, I said.

Crackers? She shouted.

Oh! No, I mean nut crackers.

Oh! My God! I thought how could you eat crackers, I wondered why you don't like your jaws and teeth, anyway I am going to help my parents out, everyone is struggling there our home is already full of relatives.

Okay, you can go, I will call you once in the night, I said.

I think there is no way to call you tonight, she said.

For few minutes, you know I can't sleep without calling you. I said.

I will try, I am unsure still but don't bother I will make it to talk for some minutes, she elaborated.

I was yet to take dinner when my phone rang the screen flashed MY LIFE CALLING. I called her back.

Hello Ghaashu…there was a lot of noise coming.

Jaanu…

Yeah! My *Ghaashu…. logsai balaie, muen jaan cha theek?* (Want to be sacrificed for you; is my life, my *Jaanu* fine?) I said lovingly and composed these words beautifully.

Yeah, I am fine, I could hear her cries.

What happened?

Jaanu grandmother is no more.

What?

She passed away.

Innalillahi wa inna alehi rajioon I murmured these Arabic lines to send her the deepest sympathy and prayed her soul to rest in peace in heavens---- a mighty reward even the micro germs desires for. Saba could be heard crying meanwhile I could hear someone calling her; she discontinued the call immediately and went off.

I too started missing her grandmother, I don't know her nor did have I seen her but Saba's emotions were enough to bring tears into my eyes. I didn't have any calls from her through the entire night and first session of the next day. She called me at improper time, I was in the class hence I wasn't able to talk with her. I ignored the call once, twice and thrice but still she remained calling me. I opted to receive if she called me again so that she may get I was in the class after hearing the lecture, she called I received and after 50 seconds I opted to disconnect the call but my finger wrongly pressed the speaker button the name *JAANU, JAANU why are you not talking* travelled everywhere and everyone laughed. I called her back when the classes went over, approximately dozens of times but the "no answer" was always the answer. I called again after few minutes, it was switched off. I can understand the reason I sent her a voice message so that she could call me immediately once switching on her phone.

No call till the late night and her cell phone was still switched off; I was horrified if her parents had grabbed her cell phone, there was no other source to catch information about her.

It looked if I had lost everything, nothing was going my way, even I missed various important classes, everything for me was faded up and I disliked each and everything coming my way. I always remained watching the phone waiting for her call.

Fine a week later, I had cocked my legs not letting others know I was going through her snaps there were dozens smarter and innocent which evoked our past, I run my hand over her face thinking where she would be and what she would be doing, neither me nor she could live without each other even for minutes. I recollected the old memories meanwhile I found my phone buzzing, it was an unknown number, and I avoid receiving. Nothing could push me to indulge myself in some other activity when my life has already booked my mind with her beautiful images, the phone buzzed for the second time but I went for it with the earlier approach. I made my mind to receive the call if my phone starts buzzing again but only to say, it is a wrong number. Same thing happened; I received the phone after third time buzzing.

Hello....it is a wron.........I couldn't complete my sentence as the voice from other end directly went to heal my pains.

Jaanu (my life)........I wished to put her words into my heart forever so that I could feel healthy; precisely her voice brushed all my sorrows.

Yeah! My sweet darling, how are you? And why you didn't call me these days is everything okay? I was shivering if I would get a negative answer.

Before she could answer she dumped me into sweet kisses, not dozens neither fifties but the number went beyond a century. That was enough clue for me to get everything was okay.

Yeah! everything is all right, last time I called you to say the battery was getting low, viewing the rush into our home and the falling snow which disturbed the electric poles got me sacred if I couldn't get my phone charged again and same thing happened, it's still dead, various days to go more as such, I was missing you being the cause I requested my friend to put you a call from her number.

That is okay, I inhaled a long breathe as long as I could, ohhhhh...*Ghaashu* you don't know what thoughts and imagines my mind went though, I was about to lose everything. Are you fine, I again put the same question that revealed I couldn't believe she is okay?

Yeah! I am fine my sweetheart, I know the reason of putting the same question again and again, don't bother the density of people is going low, I will call you once I could feel I am comfortable.

Hope so, I am eager to get your call from your own cell phone, I said.

The examinations' would be nearer now yeah? I said

Yeah! That is the problem, I am new to this field, didn't know how to get some lessons completed. Can you?

Let me know what the lesson are, I will definitely put affords.

The exams are on our heads and even ma'am hasn't completed the syllabus.

First semesters of every degree are approximately of the same character, I said.

Jaanu (my life) I could hear my brother calling me, I have to go, keep some patience until I could make a call, love you very much, loads of kisses on your face, and lips, she never kissed producing elevating confidence tones without kissing actually.

It is ok, but do say me the lessons I will teach you, I said.

That call evaporated all my sadness, I felt becoming more beefy, lives and deaths are as common as dust and they are out of control, to some extend we have wielded some control on lives but deaths are purely uncertain. People don't use to cry more when they lose their grandparents, but Saba emerged an exception not for she was attached to her but for the reason she was going to get us married, for Saba, the incident may prove hazardous and may break us apart for generations but that was not so. I got her call right before dinner, we had an extreme fine time everything looked as it was like before she could be repeatedly saying "I look ourselves going apart". The bell rang everybody rushed into the mess, Saba was too aware about our timings she hung up suggesting me to have something to eat first. After that I didn't have any calls till the next afternoon.

9

The phonic lessons

Hello... *Jaanu*

Yeah! My beauty! You are in the college right?

How can you be wrong when you are already being informed about everything, she laughed and I accompanied as usual. There is no such time when we had not laughed at the same time and same rule applies to our cries and bad times.

When you informed me? Stop trying to be a lair. I know everything about my sweetie.

Hats off!! And thanks to be so lazy and carless.

Oh! What happened?

Because I am not in college, the winter vacation, remember! Remember! You forgot?

I was just kidding to get where you are, it was the new style to know where you are actually. Once I completed the never existing sentence she burst into a giant laugh and me too.

What you are doing, the smile on my face got elevated.

Nothing, I am just holding the list of lessons ma'am hasn't covered.

Yeah! Yeah! Forward it to me, I asked, I pulled out a pen to get it noted down.

Its clauses,

Yeah! Further? I said.

Stressed and unstressed syllables', note making, precise writing, mood, gerund, active voice and passive voice, modals and some poems.

Its whole grammar dear, anything more, I asked.

No, but how could you teach me this, entire she asked.

Don't worry; let me to ask the book name.

It's English for literature for journalism. But let me know what you are going to do.

Nothing, you don't lose your nerves, it is my responsibility now to teach you, I said.

Love you my beauty, she said before kissing me, she was happy.

I kissed her too and could hear some noise from her house.

*Janu…janu…*one minute…ok byee see you later, she hung up.

Trin…trin…tri…Oh! She is calling me again I disconnected the call before it produced the third "Trin".

Hello…is everything all right.

Yeah! Brother called me, I have to go downstairs.

You should have gone without calling me again. I said.

Nope, I wanted to hear some beautiful lines from you.

Oh! How sweet, my sweetheart you gave some meaning to my life which could have been a slum without you, you are the one who let me know what loving someone is all about, you are not a simple human to me nor am I for you but someone who makes each other's hearts function to keep themselves alive.

That was as expected my *Jaanu*, only you can speak the words which could make me to live centuries more after I am dead. You made my life worthwhile with such beautiful message. Love you very much. Bye, take care.

Listen.

I am not going anywhere; I am still to go and I know have to hear kisses.

Hahaha….yeah! muahh muahh muahhh muahhh… bye take care, see you soon my princess. She did the same. I hung up.

Without wasting any time I left for the market to purchase the said text book. Her exam was important for several people around us but she was yet to revise what all she has been taught in the college. I was sacred if she fails or gets fewer marks she might be put to give a reason for and if her parents may get what we all have been into they will be unsympathetic. I wanted her to explore everything so that no one could get to know about our relationship, if you fail people will start making you prey of their nonsense comments which I never want. I never wanted our relationship to become a source for anyone to get our relation and honor mudded off. Otherwise you are not able to walk with your head up even in the streets; there were various examples of the same case. Love is a most beautiful thing in the world which continues the existence of this globe that is why I never wanted this word to be disrespected which people usually do when they fail. Love deserves respect and implementation which everybody lacks. It is common in Indian parents to care their children more when they are grown ups, love is the reason!

On a fine chill evening she called me and said.

Jaanu (my life) our examination is approaching.

You will do well, I know. But revise and I will also help you out.

I think your exams might be starting too, she said.

Why not only some days to go, the time table has already come.

Then you study yours, it's tough and needs lot of efforts, I will study on my own.

Not at any situation, we have to tighten the nuts as much as it is possible. See, each day I will teach you one topic and you have to revise it your heart out, there will be some questions from the topic to be asked to you, if you answer I will be happy to move ahead if not then you know.

It's all right, I will, what about the timing.

I will get it to you later; let me to frame a strict timetable.

One hour later, I gave her a call.

Hello *Jaanu.*

My *Ghaashu* how are you.

How many times you would say this word, yeah! As expected I am fine as usual and thanks almighty.

Everything is uncertain my dear, no one know when the time would turn around bad, not being you in front of my eyes makes me crazy to ask about your health after each passing second. You know it's a sign of love my *Ghaashu.*

How sweet my *Jaanu,* you deserve kisses for that--- muah muah muah muah muah.

Ghaashu I have come up with the time table, I hope you would compromise to get things done.

Yeah my *Jaanu* why not?

See, the class would start right after our dinner for forty minutes, you need to give me a missed call at 8: pm so that we could start. And what you have to do next is to revise it and to give me a missed call again indicating you got it properly you can call me in between if you needed any help. That means you also have to frame same timetable to get me sharp at time without any delay.

It is all right *Jaanu.*

Yeah! If you wish you could have your dinner at the time I does if not you can have once the topic is completed.

That means you don't know the timing of my dinner, yeah?

What?

Leave it.

Say please.

My dear *Jaan*, I am already following your routine since years. I really can't ignore it, I had been questioned about it but somehow I managed to associate it with my aim which let the doubt go away their minds. She said.

My *Ghaashu*, I don't know my virtues are so strong to get you as a reward; I am extremely blessed to have you as my life companion. There is no one like you in the world and yeah! How couldn't I sacrifice myself for you? My love is increasing and these things make you different from others. I love you.

Jaanu my heart is getting more and more peaceful after each passing day, and having you by my side forever is something lovable.

Ghaashu, your beauty and innocence invites me to get sacrificed for you now and forever even my life murmurs inside *"Hey Sam! Die for your Saba only once it's better than to live with some other for centuries".*

I don't know what to ask, you won.

That makes no difference; your silence tells millions of things and brings billions of happiness to my soul.

You are making me emotional; I can't even think to spend a single second without you. Love you my life.

Ghaashu, I think you go now and we will be meeting after the dinner to start our proceedings.

Ok, my *Jaanu* (my life) Love you and infinity kisses on your lips.

Love you too. Infinity kisses to your lips as well, Bye. With this I hung up.

After we were done with the dinner, there was only one thing to do without wasting much time and that was to get her going with the lessons. I called her and soon started the new phase of online phonic teaching something which was perhaps yet to be discovered.

I would teach her for one hour daily and the rules were made strict, love is not bad it doesn't mean indulging into romance only but it is something that includes sharing your ideas, happiness, joy, knowledge and skills to change each other's fortunes in the long run. I had immense respect for this word and neither wanted to get it spoiled nor to become a cause of any uncertainty.

Every day she would call me twice during the time, one, when she completes the taught lesson, second, when she was about to sleep at sharp 3: am. She really put great efforts to get things done. A doctor who wanted to become a writer was giving English lessons to a writer who wanted to become a doctor. We became hard and kept patience, there were less personal communications as at last career was something which one can't let ignored. My Saba got fully prepared for the exam and thanks for her contribution and compromise. Tomorrow is her first paper; I bowed to almighty and put a word to him for her success. I came home so that I could be with her all day on her first paper. The snow is fading and gradually the chill too is going away for a long voyage. I spoke her everything what she must need to do in the exams the night before exam.

Yes my *Jaanu,* I will follow, why not.

This is what attracts the examiner and forces him to give wealthy marks. I believe you will do well.

I need your prayers and let rest of the work on me. She had some confidence.

I forget to pray even myself because everything of my mind, heart and soul go intense hard to pray you, but note we are humans may be I can forget praying you some day but remember that day I would not be breathing.

Talk good *Jaanu*, again you are commenting the same mistake, please *Jaanu*. I would start crying.

Ghaashu ghaashu, I am sorry. I love you.

I am not going to forgive you; you have already done it several times. I hope I would never expect it to happen again, correct?

Yeah! But…

What but?

Nothing, leave it. I mean I will try to wield control over it.

Yeah! Yeah! I am here…….Ok. Ok. Saba replied to someone crying out her name loudly.

Who is she screaming your name. I said.

She's mom I need to go she is enough conservative to think it otherwise, shall I go.

There is no point to take permission from me to obey your parents, you can go my life and please sleep little early tonight and call me before going to bed.

Yeah! I will at any circumstances, bye and lots of kisses to you.

Bye… love you but do call me once more before you would sleep, I said and hung up.

10

The life taking shock

Whatis wrong today? The time has already passed eleven and the night is too numb and no call? I glanced to my phone and decided to go for a slumber. I hope I would find my phone vibrating after some minutes. As usual I placed the phone on my chest and kept my hands beneath my head and got prepared to doze.

Help! Help! Help! I rushed into my room and was astonished to see the canals of water flowing through it and Saba was found struggling for her life in the middle of the water, the mighty speed of the water was taking Saba away, her clothes were floating on the water and she was crying for help. Meanwhile I jumped into the water and found myself unhelpful as I was getting jolted out by the force of the flowing water. Soon the water got spread all over the house and everything got destructed. The speed of the water was increasing and uprooting everything coming its way, I got struck to the wall and broke my arm, she was crying for help but the force of the water never allowed me to get to her, I was trying but the water would hit me to the walls and the glasses. I wanted to rescue my life Saba but the water became cruel to force us apart and watered my might and killed my every attempt to save her. We both were crying but there was no one to hear. Surprisingly it starts raining into the house the wonder which I haven't ever seen. It's the final day for us in this world and Allah has decided to get the universe vanished in floods, my mind start thinking. It was unbelievable to see everything floating on the water like the light wooden pieces. Saba was seen nowhere now as I screamed her name but our fortune refused to follow us. Even I couldn't hear her cries, I thought she was dead.

Ghaashu….. Oh! My GOD please, get her back, I need her my God, I need her… and we apologize for the sins and crimes we had made please give us one more chance, I start crying. The speed of the water got down and the water level diminished after some minutes. Death was roaring inside and everything was completely petered. I was roaring in pain after seeing the disaster taking everything away from me. The heaven got changed into slum in no time. There was everything to cry at, the house was demolished and believe me no one could bear such ache. Stepping on the floor through the torn clothes, broken glasses, and destructed utensils I found my Saba in an awful and terrible state blooded under the bed, blood coming out of her mouth and had lost both of her eyes. I came closer to her with the mouth masked with palms, astonished, I stood on my knees and put my hands on her shoulders; there was nothing left in her, both of her eyes where nowhere, I hadn't the courage to see her, that proved beauty belongs to no one its simply meant for some time. She was struggling to say something.

Yeah! My life, please say how are you. Wake up my life, you know how much I need you, I have two eyes I will donate you one but you please don't let me alone please. The emotions and cries coming out of me can't be described in a word or two.

Jaanu (my life) someone is beating me, please help me…I think I will die.

No, my *Ghaashu*…I will not let you go, I love you. I will even turn around the orbits for you, but you please get up.

Jaanu I love you forever, never harm yourself if you did I will get pains there and I will address you if you never loved me. I love you now and always. I..I……I a.. a… am…wa… wa..i wa..it… wait…i..n wai..t.i..n..g…Y…Yo. You.

Ghashu (the light of my eyes) how can it happen, you had promised you will be obedient, don't you remember I asked you to call me before you would sleep; but you don't still, you can't go away without calling me. *Ghaashu*, we have promised to marry and live a luxurious life, please get up! I need you my life. I put her hand on my head.

Her hand starts slipping gradually and stopped on my face, I looked at her as she took a long breathe thrice before she could say I love to wait you. She was dead.

My heart went shivering and my chest went vibrating continuously, oh! My God what's it, my eyes got opened and found my cell phone vibrating over my chest. I glanced around there was no wind into my body, I was stunned, tears dropped fom my eyes, I took the cell phone the screen was twinkling to show MY LIFE CALLING.

I disconnected the call to believe little more over what I was seeing all around, I wiped out my eyes and thought once I would call my Saba I would tell her be conscious as something bad is going to happen with us. Dreams had become a source of information to me since years; this one wouldn't be counted out.

The time was 12:30 A.M; I called back.

Trin trin trin trin trin …..

Hello my *Ghaashu*

Bastard!

Yeah! Who is this? To whom I am speaking.

Get the fuck out of here, you are Sam

Yeah! I felt apart. My heart froze.

How dare you love my daughter? How you?

The alarming sentence vibrated my heart, the hairs stood up on to my body. It was a shock that never kills you at a time but kills you every second you survive. The sky fell over me. I was horrified startled to think about my Saba. I am terrified on the phone so what about my Saba who is there surrounded by his own parents like troops.

Yeah! Speak up. See, I never want to know who you are, whatever you are and from where you are I don't know nor did I want to know I just want you to forget her with immediate effect otherwise conditions would be very harsh for both of you.

Sir,

What sir! Call me a buffoon or legitimate. I don't want any respect from you.

Sir, I can understand your feelings this time I swear I would never commit such type of mistake which could become a distressing move for you and your family. I promise for that.

Fuck off! I always dislike paying attention to the psychological lectures, you don't regret what you have done, I am surprised It counts you belong to a sick family.

May be! Sir! But I am saying I will never let you down. I could hear Saba crying as somebody was hammering on her. Her cries went deep into my heart seem begging for the help, the dream produced to be a nastiest reality ever.

I don't want to hear you anymore, you sick! Talk to her for the last time as an apology. I really want to break into your house to strangulate you; you have smashed our respect and dignity and have infringed our family values.

Hello….all I could hear were cries and nothing, she was breathing very heavily of terror. *Ghaashu* I am here with you… please speak… how this all happened my *Ghaashu?* Please have a word my darling, please…I was unable to hear a word from her except cries that almost took my life away.

Jaanu (my life)

Yeah! My *Ghaashu* (the light of my eyes) please say, please, I am here with you always. My heart froze and the blood stopped running through my veins.

Jaanu (my life) are you fine my sweetheart?

Ghaashu (the light of my eyes) what can I say? Do you still care about my health when you are dying yourself? I sobbed. I am fine my sweetie. I put my head down the tears fell on the quilt.

Jaanu (my life) I am dying of pain, they practiced every punishment they know after they caught my cell phone. I don't know what to do, they don't kept my exams in mind while whacking me down, *Jaanu* my career is no more in my hands I think I can't write the exam tomorrow, they broke my arm, they even continuously struck me with the wall, her cries made me mad and unconscious and I prepared myself to rush into her house that odd time.

No, no, no, *Jaanu* (my life) please don't come, for the sake of my love please be there, you don't know how angry they are, they can do anything to you, you don't bother I will be all right after some days, you just take your absolute care, no matter what they would say or no matter how much they punish me I promise I will never let you go out of my heart. My life you are always there. My life…parents do warn us because we are doing wrong in their views but we promise to come back strong and would answer them with our strongest love. I am not a coward who will quit off from my responsibilities, na, naaa, never, I love to get in such intricate situation to overcome as a winner. I again promise we will prove ourselves the best love birds the world has ever seen and would set an example which needs courage, trust, faith, and boldness and above all the unique love and thanks almighty we possess each of the traits. We are not meant to quit, but it is a best opportunity to me to prove my true love for you. My *Jaanu* how can I forget what you have done for me, never, I love you more than before. We will come forward to come out of this mess. Love you *Jaanu*. Don't cry my dear, my words got heavier and I was hardly able to speak up. Some tears found their way direct to my mouth to get me the salty flavor; I never wanted her to suffer because of me. I really hate myself.

Her cries went deeper as I could hear someone punching her to stop speaking but she went on, her cries made it difficult to add any more word.

I was helpless to do anything, there was no point for me to go harsh, my heart almost did but somehow my mind coordinated and came up with, "if you would do, she will be in an enormous problem and you too, may be they would take any threatening decision" I kept calm but the tears refused to stop. It's the first time I have seen girls front their parents such way to keep their love alive. And you say can I ever stop loving such girl? Yes, the answer is yes; don't be shocked it's when I would forget to breathe.

Hello, her father spoke again.

Had you been a brother you have had never got yourself indulged in such cheap action.

Sir, it's entirely my mistake I apologize for my shameful move, it is none of her faults, and it is me who insisted her to build a relationship. I request you not to give her any pains and for punishment I am ready, please don't be hard over her,

I beg you, please, females are not as strong males. She would die, my Saba would die...I cried, that they would not make Saba cry anymore.

Sir, I am s.........

Stop, stop, I never told you to cry out your identity, does I? I wanted to tell him my name and profession but he was so hard to be told, he never care about me and my profession he only knew I was a biggest evil. He hung up.

My eyes totally refused even to flutter whole of the night. No one looks mine now; I perceived things in a total ambiguous way. Canals of sweat were flowing out of my body and my heart was almost to burst.

I woke up early that morning had some breakfast and went off towards her college to remain with her whole day, I wasn't sure whether her parents would allow her to attend the exam or not besides having one negative and other positive thought I proceed.

The exam was about to start, fifteen minutes to go, the sun showed itself shining after a long time but Kashmir is a place where weather changes like a tossed up coin. As soon I completed the sentence the sky brought up a blanket like clouds and it started to drizzle. My Saba was nowhere. I arm folded bowed my head and started roaming around before my eyes fell on a group of girls chirping like the birds of the dawn, I walked to them to analyze the matter as I came closer I found my Saba sitting and wiping her eyes surrounded by her friends consoling and giving her confidence. There was no other option to me except jumping and hugging Saba without introducing her friends who I was. My legs refused to balance my body when Saba looked at me, her left eye, her left eye, her left eye.......

Her left eye had turned totally green and swollen around, her left arm bandaged and hanged to her neck, her hair was totally confused not only this her face was red like blood with unlimited finger prints and scratches.

My *Ghaashu*, who did all this to my life? I looked deep into her eyes hugged her once more and start crying as loud as I could.

Jaanu, it doesn't matter I will be fine in days, and I am sorry, today I cannot hug you tightly with both of my arms, she was crying and shivering.

This sentence melted my heart and brought out countless and immeasurable tears and my arms brought her much closer. I looked at her face she does the same and we wiped off each other's tears.

The time was over now, the gatekeeper gestured to the students to come in.

Jaanu (my life) shall I go?

Off course my *Ghaashu*, come back happily, I will be waiting, best of luck.

I waited outside till she came out; her body language pledged her exam was best, I asked some of the questions, she answered correct.

You don't asked how was my exam? She said.

It's your beautiful smile which lets out all information regarding your exam, it was not good, but it was excellent I know.

But I forgot to write a two mark question, she said while making her face.

It's enough what you did in such terrible conditions, you deserve a salute, I stride four five steps forward moved back to her and saluted her, everyone around looked at us steady and intently.

Haha oh hoo thank you my life, love you.

You want anything *Ghaashu*.

Yeah! I want to be with you all time, she said innocently.

Even I want, let the right time to come you will be mine and I yours forever and no one would make us apart after, I said.

As far as your love is with me nothing will happen to me, I love you my prince. *Jaanu jaanu*..Let's move, otherwise I need to give explanations why I was late. She said while adjusting my hair by her right hand.

We need to have something you look hungry, I said.

No, not at all, I will have food in my home if they may have kept some.

Don't be so formal, come on, I hold her hand and made way towards the restaurant.

The lunch was over and that day we had world famous Kashmiri *Wazwan* dishes Saba could be seen requesting me to leave to avoid late. I brought some fruits and some medicines to get her well sooner followed by the travel to our homes.

Jaanu. Am I again going to the same people who assaulted and harassed me last night? She said looking into my eyes sitting beside me in the vehicle.

My life, you please keep patience, I will discuss this matter with my parents. It will take some time.

You are everything to me; I can wait you for years no matter how worse the situation is, she said while dropping her head into my lap.

My exams were approaching too and one never wants such tragedies to happen before to offer pains and cries from both sides. Next day I found my phone ringing in the balcony it was an unknown number which I ignored but the consecutive calls made me to pick one to answer and get to know what the matter was.

Hello….

Yeah! Who is this?

Sam, I am *Zahida*, Saba's neighbor and she wants to talk with you.

What...Really? I disconnected the call and called back. That phone call lashed all appall out of me.

Hello...

Hello *Jaanu*.

Hello *Ghaashu*, how are you.

I am fine, and more over I am getting better now.

Do they question you about anything? I said.

Not, but their staring told everything itself, she said.

Ghaashu I don't know why I think the world is no more mine, why I think my heart wouldn't beat anymore, why I think everyone is my enemy, why I think I will not wake up in the morning, why I think my soul is dead, why I think you would never meet me again and why I think I should ask you what I am thinking my sweetheart? I said in a typical Shahrukh Khan sobbing style which makes everyone cry.

I believe we would get married one day to live a prosperous and handsome life full of love, care and respect. Let them to know you are a doctor, they will accept you with both hands.

I am ready to do anything for you, I promise.

I need your support and nothing else, we will show each and everyone love makes careers rather it spoils.

I don't know what future will come up with, will there be a time for us to live happily or will it become something which would force us apart, I don't know why I think so.

We will make out of this mess, I have very limited time to talk with you, I am not allowed even to go outside of the main gate either.

Ghaashu, you just go, I love you, I don't want you to suffer any more for me, I said.

I never want to hung up but I have to, you know, I would give calls to you now and then from this number.

Ok, my *Ghaashu,* love you so much. Bye.

Love you lots of kisses to you. I kept the phone touched to my ear waiting she would disconnect but she was waiting for the same from me.

Ghaashu, ok take care, disconnect the call now. I said.

No I can't, I haven't any courage to go away from you, I request you to disconnect.

Even I can't, I said and consumed another few minutes deciding who would disconnect but no one did.

Ghaashu, I have an idea. I said

What?

I will just count one, two, three up to ten and what we need to do is press the red button at ten to disconnect the call, ok?

Haha, she flashed into a short laugh proving there is no more energy in my girl followed up by saying, ok.

Ready?

Yeah!

One, two, three, four, five, six, seven, eight, nine, and ten, no one disconnected.

Jaanu, why you did not disconnect? She said

Ghaashu, I can also ask you the same question, I said.

Let's do it once more, one, two, three........................... ten and we hung up.

Next day I again called *Zahida* who received after three full calls.

Hello...

Yeah! *Zahida* how are you?

Fine and what about you?

Fine by the blessings of our creator, tell me how my Saba is.

Oh! My God! I can't believe what has happened to her; hell to such parents who even don't cared about her life. At last she is a lady Sam they should grow up.

I can't say anything, I am restless and burning into pains, I never wanted myself to become a source to her pains. I said with emotions running down.

You want to talk her? She put me a question.

I never think a time would ever come when I would refuse talking to her, but I don't want you to be caught into the same net otherwise it would be more difficult for us to communicate, you are the only source to get me to her and I didn't want to lose it any way. I said.

I will definitely make her to talk with you later, she said.

Listen, I am going to college I have something to ask you, see, she has lost everything, the charm and the strength and it is very difficult to pass days when your exams are running so I have put a word to the fruit seller who would supply fruits to Saba every day, I request you to get those fruits to her someway without asking anything about me.

That is fine but she would definitely ask who is giving it to her, but I can handle, she said.

Thank you, please do go to her home to say I am leaving and be waiting on the balcony I would be coming.

Ok, I will.

Ok, sister bye.

Bye.

I got changed and was ready to leave for my college when my phone was heard ringing, the screen flashed "Sister Zahida", I disconnected and called back.

Hello….it was my Saba.

Yeah *Ghaashu*, I am on the way and will be there soon please be there in the balcony.

Ok, *Jaanu*, how much time will it take, my parents are here and today they look in some ferocious mood, she said as I could found terror in her words.

Only, five minutes.

Ok. I am waiting, she said

After fine five minutes I got there and looked out of the glass and gestured goodbye, and gave some flying kisses.

She did but she could not do it with both of her hands.

I got another call as I passed her house.

Hello…

Yeah *Ghaashu* say…

Jaanu, I am sorry I wasn't able to say you goodbye with both of the hands, I got emotional again.

Ghaash----You don't make me emotional anymore you will get fine very soon, my prayers are with you always.

Some time passed and Kashmir changed its color and fragrance, the sky looks clear and the sun is turning hot and fresh. Her exams are finished and so are mine.

The weather got changed, Kashmir was moving to other silhouette which makes my beloved Kashmir the most beautiful place on earth and that was the spring. Little buds were coming out of the twigs shining that looked if the diamonds were gleaming on the trees. The little different colored innocent flowers shining on every fruit tree was the sign of new fragrance to our state. The breeze also took off its flight to kiss the unlimited treasures of heaven Kashmir to offer freshness and happiness to enormous souls and millions of hearts. The New Year in Kashmir starts now when each individual looks fresh and confident especially the older fellows who almost spent whole of the winter only in the rooms with the Kashmir typical earthen pot beneath the fern giving them the odor of the summer. Everything looked new and shining right from the tinny leaves to the giant forests, the chirruping of the birds in the dawn and the children going back to school in the colorful uniform, the gardens generating perfumes from the never ending species of flowers, the farmers back to their workplace with the pair of oxen walking before them and the yoke on their shoulders adds Kashmir as a heaven. The migration of different kinds of birds to take pleasure and get fed on the apple, walnut and mulberry gardens makes it one of the supreme places to visit. The sound created by the flowing water from the canals, rivers, and other water bodies which were dumped under the snow has now found a reason to get the immense agriculture fields irrigated. One cannot forget to say good bye to the room heaters blankets and earthen pots and welcome room coolers and fans back to their business. It looks wonderful to get off the caps from our head and wear slippers again. Everyone looked thin and less beefy thanks to the sweaters, jackets and thermo cots which protected us from the creeping chill and made us enough large. The clouds are nowhere and welcome to the stars, moon and the sun which made themselves visible after a long time. The breeze adds its speed and makes the leaves to move like a pendulum but everything was out of me but it was for those who are happy and free from any kind of discomfort. All the things which I described never gave me the pleasure, the wind for me doesn't look so fresh, the flowers never seem shining and the water bodies looks of no use, not having her happy drives me in the list of unsound minded people and makes all the things worthless to me.

One day sitting in laboratory one of my friends messaged me on my phone, "I hope you will be fine, the result of your Saba is coming tonight".

I desperately waited for the evening, approximately at 11:30 I checked and found my Saba has got 71% of marks for the first year where maximum of the students got in the fifties. This was the greatest news for my soul which has been living in the dark shadows since past two months my chest got broad enough with proud.

Next morning sitting in the library I got a news paper and start reading the back page where the university had come up with different toppers from different colleges. Soon my eyes fell on Handwara college where I could see my Saba at the top with a cute smile. I glanced here and there kissed her photo and cut it to put into my pocket. Meanwhile my phone rang, and the screen gave the name "Sister Zahida" calling

Hello, I spoke as loud as I could.

Hello, it was not my Saba.

How are you?

I am fine.

Congratulations! It is not for Saba but it heartily goes for you who stood by her side and guided her besides these conditions. Saba told me the whole secret of her success. I have seen people loving but the way you are doing it is exceptional and unique, my prayers are with you always.

Thank you, but where is she. I asked.

I am sorry to say she is no more allowed to be with me, because of my phone. Her parents' doubts are soaring negatively thinking I am insisting her and getting both of you closer. She said.

But is she fine?

Yeah! She is fine, but her parents hate her now, they don't care about her anymore, they even didn't celebrate her success rather they were staring at her whole day.

Can I talk to her this time or the other?

Very difficult, I may say it is impossible as well. But I will try if I got some chance.

Thank you for your patience, I said.

Take care; I am by your side bye.

Ok. Bye. She hung up, she was not my Saba who could wait for me minutes long to disconnect the call, it was some other. I thought inside.

Her success gave coolness to my burning heart, these were unbearable pains not talking or seeing the person whom you love this much and something no one wants. I can't believe the past days when both of us were close and playing and gossiping with each other, it is the matter of time and situations which can play anything even with those who are made for each other. This love is very unlawful it goes to someone so easy and to someone it comes after a lot of struggle and to someone it remains all about to struggle till they struggle to live and to someone their death become their love. I am not now a member to be counted in the first group but surely there is a chance to be a member of the second.

Several weeks passed, to spend each day in the college looks if I was put behind the bars. Nothing was going in my mind even at times I forgot my name also. How is my Saba? What she will be eating? How she will be living? And what she will be doing? All were the questions to which no one could answer me.

I was left with one option to call Sister *Zahida* to ask her about the correspondence, she accepted to help my letters to get to her.

One evening I went to write a letter for her.

#. *My dearest lady,*

First and foremost I congratulate you for your success which I celebrated in a unique way without you, sorry for that. It was something which healed my heartily gashes after long time. Thank you for this. I hope our creator must have kept my girl all right these days. The night is numb, the stars, the moon and the Milky Way seems praying for our good time. Living apart from each other drives me mad and unconscious, the world is tasteless without you and the day I doesn't see or talk you is the day which diminishes my life by years. I wish I could be the flower and you could be the butterfly coming to suck my blood to live your life healthy. My days never pass without thinking and praying you and if I would ever do it today I am sure I would never see my tomorrow. I wish you could be here to jump into my lap and surround my ribs by your soft skinned shiny arms to bring back those beautiful days. I am missing you I want to gaze your big brown eyes with curved eyelashes and the pink lips which gave me warmth in the winters. My heart is burning inside and there is no medicine to cure it except your tight embrace. I don't know why love came to us in such a terrible face and I don't know when my wounds are going to heal. You are seen everywhere and I use maximum of my time talking to your snapshots. This bad time will go off quickly we can't let such facets out if we love each other this much. I love you more than the previous second and I hope you would never be unkind to yourself. I hope you are taking the fruits regularly and I hope there is some improvement in your health. I have good news for you my life, you always said you want a big house to live in after your marriage, yeah! The construction has been started to get it ready before we will get married. It is the starting; I have to fulfill every dream of my sweetheart. I am waiting to know your kind reply and do not forget to put lots of kisses packed into your letter. You are not any less than my creed you are always in my heart which beats for you. Love you so much my Ghaashu.

Yours loving Sam

Days passed giving the same pain and ache. I could hear the post man calling me as I went out; he asked my name and kept the parcel in my hand. I opened and found a big white sheet written to full and noticed the writing faded up at some

212

places perhaps because of water drops. It was from my Saba and I sat down to read it.

#. The light of my eyes,

This letter provided magical greenery to my heart. I believe you are the only person who is happy over my results, my parents never did. My Jaanu, I wonder if I am living around the same walls which loved me before getting into relationship. My life has been changed forever in the past two months. I am not even allowed to go anywhere. I don't want to stay here; everyone is against me and humiliates me every day. Jaanu, last night my brother and father kicked me ferociously for preparing the vegetables less tasty. My jaanu I am suffering from cold since a week but no one dare even to ask me for a medical checkup, to visit even the threshold of the main gate has become a dream for me and it was about two months before when I was allowed to open the window of my room. I am not allowed to go to college anymore. I am being offered meals like a prisoner and I am being treated like a beast. I couldn't find that much love anywhere, if you utilize your time talking to my snaps which I too do laying into the corner of my room and crying for you. My jaanu, my parents think I love a nothing man, they don't know you are a doctor nor they want to know anything about you, the day they would know, I believe we would get married happily. My life, all my writing materials was set to fire. I had written beautiful poems for you but they are no more. I am dying here and no one helps. Jaanu, I am struggling to write tears are dropping on the sheet and I am sorry as they faded up the writing. But I promise I would never cry staying with you in that big beautiful house even if you hit me. I love you always.

Always in your heart
Yours Saba

After reading the letter I forgot where I was some more tears dropped on the letter and got the writing faded up more. I threw my hands into my hairs to pull them out. How and when are you going to forgive yourself if someone's life is ruined because of you? I questioned myself and found the answer quiet latter. *"I need kill myself to find her forgiven"* but it was not the perfect solution I came up with, if I did her life would be even worse. I sat down to write a letter to her but writing letters would never rescue her anymore it needs some practical work. How helpless I am? My mind froze and my eyes stun. I checked my watch; the time was 12:45 pm meanwhile my phone rang.

I pulled out Nokia 1100; the black and white screen flashed Sister Zahida Calling.

Hello…..*jaanu*, I could hear breathing sounds.

Yeah my *Ghaaashu* how are you. I was delighted to hear her charming voice after a long time.

Jaanu, they are going to marry me. What shall I do? *Jaanu* they warned me not to tell this news to you. I don't want to live here, please take me somewhere we can be alone.

What? This news came to me like a death and stunned me my eyes came out and my face changed like a fireball. I was immovable I couldn't speak for some time; it looked if my heart was coming to my mouth.

Yeah! What shall I do? Please tell me. My brother has told his friend to marry me as soon as possible who is working in the police department with him. They will be coming next week. I am dying my sweetheart; I don't know what to do. She was crying.

Nothing will happen, your *Jaanu* is with you all time, I summed up these words in some way but each of my senses wasn't coordinating me.

I am very frighten, I am sure they would pummel and scourge me if I ignore.

Ghaashu

Yeah, she said.

I was dumb to say anything accept to produce little sounds meaning nothing.

Jaanu, please say what shall I do, please. She said.

Ghaashu, it's enough now, you just get ready to elope, I would come there just now and we would go out to live with each other peacefully forever, I said.

No, *Jaanu*, it's not possible; I am not allowed to go out of my room how could it be possible, she was crying.

Give me your fathers' cell number, I will beg him not to make us apart, I said

No, *jaanu* he will kill me before you can do so, I have already promised him not to tell it to you.

Ghaashu, please you come out of your home some way and rest depends on me, I said.

Jaanu I have some other idea I think I would tell the boy everything about our love, she said.

Ghaashu… ghaashu I tried to tell her one more thing but the call was disconnected. I called back but the mobile was switched off.

I have some other ideas; I cannot let the person suffer alone who has sacrificed lots of things for me. I went home to discuss this matter with my parents.

After the dinner was completed, I requested my mother to stay with me for some time. My father also came and joined the party.

Papa….papa….I stopped I haven't the courage to tell him my career was hanging, I had no job in my hand to fed my wife and children and second the person whom I was going to tell was the strict and hardest father in the world.

I know you want to tell something about your studies, I trust you, so please go ahead, my father said.

Papa it's not all about studies, it's something else. I was shivering inside. I knew he would kill me but I wanted them to know I love somebody more than myself and she needs my cooperation to live happily once again.

There is a girl, there is a girl, whom…whom

Whatever you want to say please don't say I love her or something else.

Papa, I don't want to say I love her, but I have to say I want to marry a girl who is suffering and has sacrificed a lot for me, I can't live without her, she is my life.

What???? Are you mad? Get out you ridiculous, get lost! You are at the peak of your career and you want to get it watered? You hurt me.

Papa I don't ask you to get us marry, I promise I will marry whenever you would ask but only with her, she can't face all these hardships alone after all I love her and my heart beats for her.

What the hell are you saying, go and admit yourself into a mental hospital, do you have a handsome job? Or do you think you can feed your children and wife. I want to make him a great doctor and he wants something else. He looked at my mother.

I don't want to marry now, I want it after I would get some job at least you can put a word to her parents so that her suffering and torment would get reduced, I beg you papa, please I said touching his feet.

It is not a genuine issue, who the hell that girl is, girls are very corruptive, they only destructs lives and see, it's the peak of your career forget her as soon as possible otherwise the only thing you will get from me is something very painful, he said angrily.

216

I can't live without her; I can only after I sleep forever.

You non sense you don't know how to talk with your parents, with this the shelling and bombardment of punches, kicks and slaps started. My mom was not an exception she also joined him until I was unconscious and that day they showed they have in them the traits of beasts.

They hammered me so hard even the food into my stomach refused to be there anymore, I started vomiting and with this I was carried to my bed. The pains and the injuries to my body didn't let me to sleep all night I wanted to elope with her to such a place where only our creator could reach but I never wanted my brothers and sisters to suffer. I was the eldest, I love them all and I had a lot of responsibility to make their life worthwhile. To leave my Saba was out of question but to leave my parents and siblings was something which raised questions what to do next. Saba was going to get engaged in some days and my destiny lies in these days and the decision of my life lies in the way these days would turn.

Next morning, I woke up early and left my home, where was I going I didn't know. There was only one way to get help and yeah if you have trust you would get helped by almighty in such a way that no one can overcome you and there is no one who can help you if you are forsaken let your trust be enough strong. Nobody could help us except our creator.

My head hung in distress and pain, tears rolling down if it was drizzling, made my legs to a mosque to pray almighty for my help nights and days he was the only source to help me when there was no one by my side. I went in after a bath and ablution and decided to spend some days in his ways until I would get some happiest news.

I shed tears as much as I could, bowed in front of him and recollected all the good times we had.

"My Allah, you are the greatest, we can't bear your punishment, please help us in this worse time, I know we are sinners we apologize, you order things to happen and only you can stop them. There is no one mine except her in this world, please save her. I can sacrifice anything in your ways for her. Three days passed and I hardly slept, begging almighty to give my Saba back I found some inner courage and happiness seems to kiss my feet, waiting for the call restlessly which would decide my future. Conservatism has much power than anyone and I am sure only God is above their decisions. Our villages and Indian culture is still full of this concept which had already taken millions of lives, love is not any bad, it is the meeting and understanding of two hearts which are ready even to sacrifice themselves for the happiness of each other. Where do you people find a fault in it? But these people will never understand nor will they allow anyone to understand it. I knew my creator is with me, he will not let me down, I trust my prayers.

Full seven days passed and my eyes have now forgotten the concept of dryness, they are red and about to burst, my hands and my legs never sported me, my eyes were going down in the socket the beard and my nails were growing too long. The confusing hair would tell my every story. There was no energy in me as I had hardly taken any meals, my stomach went too close to my spinal cord but I never lost the battle, the consumption of every second in almighty's ways gradually promised I was pulling my Saba back to me.

After a long time my phone start ringing which ends my long lasting wait, I checked and the screen was twinkling like a star with the name "Sister Zahida" it was the call in which my life, happiness and fate was buried. My hands were not working anymore; I disconnected the call and called back.

Hello...

Hello my sweetheart, say *Alhamdulillah* (thanks to almighty) she looked pumped up.

Alhamdulillah, I said.

I told him everything about you and me. She said very happily.

Thanks my almighty, I was pumped up, I punched my fist in the air in delight but fell down, the happiness I felt inside was immeasurable, I wanted to know what happened.

Jaanu my parents forced me to get in to him and they accompanied, I wasn't able to ask him anything for first thirty minutes, I only asked about his age because he was looking very nasty, he was thirty four.

You didn't speak.

No, I only asked him only one question and that too of age and spent maximum times wiping my eyes. But he couldn't understand my condition.

When you asked him about me, I asked.

After thirty four minutes my parents went outside, he said he liked me and wanted to marry, I followed by saying all about you and he turned red and humiliated.

I have never seen girls doing so for their love I may have seen but only in movies. I love you my *Ghaashu,* I wanted to embrace her but she was very far.

I love you too, my *Jaanu* where are you it looks pretty silent.

I am on the college terrace; I didn't tell her I am in the mosque since a week to get you back.

But how far should I remain silent, I had three things in my life, one was my career second was Saba and third were my parents. It was very hard to miss anyone among them. If my career is good our life is good and our life will only be good when parents' prayers are backing us.

Two months later……

Mr. Sam come out here is another letter to your name even the postman knows me well now.

He handed me over the letter went quickly into the room and started reading it.

#. *My loving Sam*

It took days to love you, it took weeks to understand you, it took months to make you my own but it would take my life to forget you. Sitting in the old corner of my house crying for my fate but today I would make sure there are no teardrops on the letter. This corner is everything to me now and I have approximately spent whole of my time crying and talking to the imprints you laid over my heart. Jaanu, I am being forced and threatened to get married immediately, they have shown me approximately fifteen boys since I called you last time accurate thirty seven days before which I ignored and they went on hammering me. Jaanu, I have no energy left to front such wild family. Sometimes my chest goes paining hard which stops me to think for another minute of life, it started from the day they kicked my chest and stomach hard, and still I am not allowed to go to the doctor. My Jaanu I haven't seen the sunlight since months, I hope when you would write me you would describe the nature in your letter, I hope your writing will do it as my eyes do. Jaanu, wasn't I telling you I want to explore the world? How bad I am who never thought one day I will not be allowed even to open the window of my room. But I have a unique gift which sails me round the world hundred times a day, even centuries to spend in imprisonment are lesser for his single glimpse and that is you. Nothing is out of my ways till you are by my side. I love you.

Yours Saba

My Saba was suffering from pain, hell to them. I couldn't write a letter filling it with the medicine names she must took to cure; I gave a whip to my eyes and called Sister Zahida immediately after reading the last word.

Hello...

Yeah, hello, how are you. She said.

I am fine, are you at your home?

Off course, say.

Saba is suffering from chest pain, you please give her the phone I will suggest her some medicines.

Even I told her parents let her to visit a doctor but they ignored saying she is making dramas. She said.

I was stunned by such answer, but can you get me to her? I said.

I will give you a call that time, all right?

Okay, I said.

After fine fifteen minutes my phone rang half, it was her. Hello...

After listening the cute hello, my mouth automatically cried out, my *Ghaashu,* is my *Ghaash's* chest paining?

Yeah my *Jaanu,* she cried.

Nothing to worry my *Ghaashu,* just tell me the symptoms so that I can suggest you some medicines, she spoke everything and I suggested her some tablets and liquid.

Jaanu. I cannot afford, she said in a pity tone.

I know you aren't allowed to go outside, I will ask sister Zahida to get it for you.

I don't mean that, *Jaanu,* I haven't seen even a penny since months and my purse is empty, her sobbing dies me.

That was a life taking sentence, my fingers refused to hold my phone anymore. I was dumped into silence nothing came out of my throat for dozens of seconds. My *Ghaashu* it is no issue when your *Jaanu* is alive, I will talk to Sister Zahida to give her account number so that I can transfer some money into that.

No, no, no, I will do something; you need lots of money to stay in city. I will tell someone to give me credit for some time.

My *Ghaashu*, you don't look good when you argue, I struggled to ask the sentence further my throat went dry and my eyes got full of tears.

My *Jaanu*, you don't cry please I will get fine soon it is a matter of time. Even you don't look handsome when you cry. She said.

My *Jaanu*, one more thing, please pen down a cell number.

Which cell number, I said.

Jaanu, last night I heard my parents discussing about my marriage and some way I found that boys number with whom they are planning to marry me.

That was even horrific, the wind looks dried up into my lungs, what I have to do I managed to say.

You just call him and tell him everything, so that my pains and ache will get a break. I could hear she was sobbing.

Ok, she uttered the number and I penned it down. I never thought what would happen if her parents would come to know it but I would try to convince that boy lovingly so that he may not cheat. I thought inside.

I had never thought my love would produce only pains for her if I would have I had never loved her, my Saba was tortured every possible ways but she never made me to feel alone, she always cares me besides being herself burning into the mighty fire each day.

Okay, my *Ghaashu* see you soon. Everything will get fine. I said.

Byee, see you my life.

I went to the bank and transferred three thousand rupees after calling Sister Zahida to get her account number.

I was caught into a what to do condition, it was easy to call a boy telling him not to marry the girl whom I love very much but its consequences' were uncertain and may be very dangerous. Anyway I have to do something very soon in such a condition when no one is mine except my Saba, I called him and he picked the call in after four rings.

Hello...

Yeah! Hello, who is this?

Hello I am Sam, the man whose life and career is in your hands. I said emotionally.

I am not getting you, speak clear, he said.

I mean you are going to tie a knot with a girl, yeah?

Obviously, it is what men and women do, she is a writer and I have already accepted her but besides this I am going to see her after days.

You love her. I said

Oh! Why not, love happens its easy first let her to come here.

Does she love you? I put him a question.

We haven't seen one another yet but as expected she will and she has to.

Can I ask you something? I said

Ok, go ahead.

See, I love Saba and she loves me ten times more than I love her, we have been in a relationship since years, I am not any threatening or warning you but I am begging you to please give me my Saba back. It is a big and emotional story which can't be summed up in one or two sentences. We can't live without each other.

What you want me to do, he said.

Please do something showing a lack of interest in her which is expectable by both of the families. I again beg you, please don't mention my name or anything which could be life horrible for us; if you do they will kill her. I said.

Okay, my brother I can understand, I will handle the matter, best of luck for both of you. He said.

It is my request, I said.

Okay, don't take any pains, bye. He hung up,

Days are going by and Kashmir is changing its colors, there couldn't be someone as unlucky as my Saba is who is even not allowed to open the window of her room to see what is happening around. She lives in such a state which is an example of beauty where people from different corners of the world come and enjoy but everything she was seeing were the same windows and same darkness dominating the room. I took a pen and a copy to write her about the beauty of Kashmir, she loves nature and may be this letter becomes a source of her happiness and smile.

My life

My Ghaashu, I have called that boy who agrees to do what I said. I want to die before I could write what I have planned to write you today. You made me to die by saying you haven't opened the window of your room and there is no one except me who could tell you what is happening outside, I know you love nature and these days our beautiful Kashmir has come up with such a beauty which no one wants to go out forever. My Jaaanu, month's back it was white and then turned to green and now it is turning to yellow. The vast trees are letting down the yellow components on the surface. The fields are harvested, men and women are carrying the harvested paddy on their shoulders and the cattle are feeding on the never ending landscapes and meadows. The oriental plane trees known as Chinar trees are firing up with their red surface and the leaves cries seeing somebody walking over them. The ground looks reddish and the women could be seen collecting the twigs and the leaves to use it as a fuel in the coming winter. The apple, walnut and mulberry gardens have nothing to feed the birds except the yellowish leaves and some rotten fruits over them. The leaves fell from the trees continuously and it looks if yellow snow is falling from the skies. The birds look going thinner, the parrots are seen nowhere. Crows, sparrows and other birds started to build their nests under the roofs of different houses as the trees went bald, the new days have come up with the mighty ants travelling in a queue emerging from a deep hole into the ground with the stuff into their mouths getting ready to face the other side of Kashmir seasons the whitey winter. The cicadas could be screeching into the yellow trees mostly faded making us clued up about the winter season. The air has started to bring some coldness into it the temperature has gone down and the water in the rivers and lakes has started gone colder. The leaves on the ground add the beauty of Kashmir, it looks if yellow and red carpets are stretched along the ground ending nowhere. The nights have other ideas as the crickets started stridulating into the fences and walls and the owls could be heard hooting over the roofs and into the trees. The stars look fading day after day and the moon could be seen even in the daytime pleading the sun to give her some light to help out the travelers and other birds and animals to travel on the roads, streets and the forests during nights. My Jaanu you are the moon and I am the traveler who is helped by your brightness to find the way to your heart. I swear I have seen moon talking with me in my lap, I swear I have seen moon laughing into my lap and shedding tears for me. I am seeing moon in light.

Yours forever
Sam

Two weeks later in the class room my phone rang and I silenced it in a hurry without seeing who it was. The moment I placed it in my pocket it again started ringing, I saw the screen showed, "Sister Zahida".

I went outside the class after taking permission from the teacher.

Hello… my voice was too loud I went out of the department.

My *Jaanu*, where are you? She said and she looked very upset.

What happened my *Ghaashu*. I said.

My *Jaanu*, I will die, I will surely die now. She was crying loudly.

My *Ghaashu*, what happened, I will never let you to go away what is the matter. I said.

No, *jaanu*, you cannot do it now, I cannot say what happened to me but I can say I want to leave you now, my *Jaanu*, why you love me so much if you can marry a better girl than me. I could hear her crying wasn't stopping.

Ghaashu what are you saying? Please tell me what happened, please.

Why should I tell to make you feel sad, I don't want, please go away, I don't deserve you now.

Jaanu, please say, for your love's sake, I am here with you *Ghaashu*, please.

I am the happiest girl, I know one of my promises will get fulfilled I know I will die before you, her cries hurt me inside.

Please don't say like this, it doesn't suit with such a girl who is my life, I know we would die with hand in hand, I couldn't stop my emotions now, I burst in a loud cry.

No one could stop me from fulfilling that wish my sweetheart. She made me mad with her cries.

I beg you to say my *Ghaashu,* I can do anything for you, I said while going to and fro in restlessness.

My *Jaanu,* yesterday night my parents came into my room like troops with washing bats, canes and sticks and assaulted me after getting you had threatened that boy to marry me, my *Jaanu,* they made me worth die, they even didn't get pity over me while ironing my thighs and arms. They never thought of women hood when they shaved my head, my *Jaanu,* my mother even tried to burn my parts which separates me from you and my brothers were continuously pulling down my pajama to burn me, my *Jaanu,* there is nothing to say more, my *Jaanu* your Saba has no hair on her head and her legs and thighs are burnt, my *Jaanu* I am not any beautiful now, my chest and stomach is paining hard, my *Jaanu,* I will die. My *Jaanu,* you still love me *Jaanu?*

The light got off from my eyes, and the sky fell over me, I can't even think humans exists on earth, my eyes came out and turned red, my whole body starts shivering and the phone fell from my hand, there was nothing left to do nor to say except punching my chest and pulling out my hairs wildly. And I cried I am coming, I am coming.

Such situation never allows thinking of next day; I don't know what I was doing as I left to her house without telling anybody where I would go. The titan watch round my wrist showed it was 11:30 am, Friday. I planned to go to her house and talk to her parents.

The handkerchief in my hands turned totally wet of tears as I rushed into the vehicle to take me there in two hours time. I was mum and tears rolling down, one of the passengers asked me if somebody close to me had died and there was no reason to tell him anything except to reply in affirmative. He consoled me and tried to bring me out of the thought but the reason was some other. I got out of the vehicle and went into an inn where I could change, there were some policemen who stare me wiping my eyes and going into the inn. I put on a black pant and black coat which never suited my conditions but I tried to look like a professional so that her parents may never think I was a driver or any conductor. My heart was full of tears rather than blood; today I would tell them your daughter had never loved a driver but a doctor. At last my *Ghaashu's* sufferings had an end today, it was all my mind was packed with. The Friday prayers are about to begin a giant blasting sound stuck my ears as I came out, it was a bomb blast in the main market soon people could be seen running here and there crying help! Help! Help! The market was disturbed and there was a great hustle bustle all around, the dust went skies as I also opted to run.

I could hear someone screaming, "Catch the black dressed man; Catch him! Catch him! He has changed his dress, I saw him in T-Shirt and jeans few minutes before"

I don't paid attention I looked behind to see three big helmeted policemen chasing me.

Stop you Bastard! Stop! I don't know why they were trying to stop me; meanwhile they caught me for which I asked the reason.

Where from you are?

See, I am a local boy perusing MBBS from Srinagar, I have lots of trouble to solve being the reason to go to my home and you please let me go. I elaborated everything clearly.

Was it important for you to change the dress to look like a bridegroom? You Shit! Tell the reason fast. One of the policemen shouted at me.

They hold my hand followed by wearing the handcuffs saying you are under arrest and dragged me down. The word roamed into my mind, Fridays had become a sign of terror both for the corps and the civilians but this one targeted me.

Numberless corps surrounded me and was taken to the local police station for further investigation.

And you are responsible for the blast? One of the interrogators with long hair and a fat stick in his hand told me.

No sir, I don't know anything, I am a medical student as I forwarded him my college card.

Even doctors can do such type of wildish activities; we have few examples in the past. He told in a deepest of his tones.

What you do here? He said.

I am a local boy, I had an urgent work someone is waiting me. I said.

I don't think you could be having as much urgent work as you did, and someone who is waiting you Is death and punishment itself a reward for what you have done. His voice went roaring.

I was on the path to my home, I request you to please release me I don't know anything.

You were on the way to home, yeah? There was no need to get your dress changed to look like a professional; you should have gone in the casuals as well.

It is a very big tale, you can't understand, I spoke the truth.

That is what we want. He punched the desk and said these words.

I was assaulted and humiliated whole night I was beaten wildly, I cried for Saba to help me but no one was there. They made me to answer various stupid questions to put me behind bars the next day.

They checked my phone but didn't found anything dangerous accept the contacts of my friends.

Saba was in my heart waiting me to come; all my contacts with the world were disconnected as I was dragged into a dark room with a single window. Next day my father came with different proofs and evidences to prove I was a doctor but still the imprisonment for a year was announced. I was behaved if I was an animal no one cares I was innocent. I don't know what my Saba would be thinking, yesterday during the torture she called me at least fifty times but the bullshits never allowed me to receive her call. I was beaten continuously and was threatened to be implicated to a much worse case if I would not give them bribe, one of the torture experts a fat man with his stomach one feet out of his body electrocuted me for two hours until he made me agree to pay two lakh as bribe, we had no other source of income in our home except my father who normally earned ten thousand rupees per month. My father sold the land and for the remaining amount there was nothing to sell. My mother had no gold or silver to sell. One day my father came to meet me in the lockups and told they have sold the only piece of land and have managed one lakh fifty thousand rupees but fifty thousand was still short. I was helpless and my parents were upset what to do next. The policemen treated me very badly and always threatened me to go harsh if I would not give the bribe. It was approximately three months now in jail I missed my Saba very much and could always dream about her. I had various nasty dreams about her but I trusted she would be fighting for me. Whole of our village knew about me now, one day my father again visited me he had brought fried chicken because he know I was the biggest meat eater. What he told me was shocking, he told me that some days before a beautiful lady came to our home and gave me fifty thousand rupees when asked what it was she never told anything but she told "uncle I heard you need fifty thousand rupees so I thought I would help you out, I am Sam's best friend". I knew she could be my Saba but how she managed such huge amount was surprising. My father gave the whole amount to the police officer who wrote a liberty note and told I will be given freedom only after completing one full year as the decision has already been made. My father was dismayed on his decision as we had already paid the huge amount as a bribe. My MBBS degree was at its last stage even my friends and teachers spoke about my justice but no one paid attention to them. The nights and days were one and the same thing for me in the darkest room. One fine morning the police officer gave me a letter; I opened it and found it was from sister zahida.

My brother Sam

I was shocked to hear this news some days before, but you don't lose hopes we are with you. Saba couldn't eat or drink without you, she was faint after hearing you are behind the bars, but I have consoled her you would get justice in no time. Once I heard your father needed fifty thousand rupees to release you I went to say the same news to Saba. She was getting mad but she collected everything she had the diamond ring, the golden chain, and some earrings and all the gifts and told me to sell them. After two days I sold them for fifty one thousand rupees and went to your home with that amount, your father was shocked but I told him I am your friend. I hope you and Saba will be living together very soon. Her parents are still searching a boy for her, even I am a witness to three you don't worry your Saba is enough courageous and bold she would never let it to happen. We are waiting you, come soon.

Zahida

After collecting the bribe they harassed me less but treated me the same way they were doing. I was burst and exhausted my body had no energy, I cried for my Saba but unfortunately she never came to console me. Money was the only thing she hadn't sacrificed but today she left no example how much she loved me, her love can't be compared to anyone in this world, I cried as much as I could but the darker walls of the prison had no effect or mercy on me. A full year of pains, misbehave, harassment, assaults and tortures was about to get completed, one of my senior fast friends came to meet me the last day, he was emotional and so was I. He gave me twenty thousand rupees and told to buy a diamond ring for your Saba on the engagement. He also warned me never leave such a masterpiece. I refused to collect telling him I had already placed an order but he went telling me the amount had a life time maturity and went off. I took the letter in my hand which Zahida had sent approximately seven months before and got emotional but overall I was delighted to get released to meet Saba.

How delighted my Saba would be when she would see me coming to her home to seek for our marriage? How beautiful my Saba would look after wearing the diamond ring. Our marriage seem kissing our feet now. Let this miserable night to pass, there is going to be roses under our feet henceforth, how momentous my life would be spending it with that person who adds her rights and even blood to make it colorful. I will give her a very better life full of prosperity and dignity. I start thinking about the cooking she has talked me about and it looked funny as I found my lips going wider. There was no place left empty in my mind without my Saba for whom it is working. The night didn't give me any sleep I remain busy thinking how beautiful our life is going to be.

In the early morning a team of troops and some other formal dressed people including my parents came close to the giant ironic gate to open it to get me released after accurate one year, I hugged my mother and father who kissed me on my forehead and I went on with them, I didn't forgot to purchase the ordered diamond engagement ring.

Everyone could be seen visiting me after I reached home, the night spent was very talkative giving reasons for going behind the bars and all the fuss. But I remained waiting for the next day to turn my life's beautiful day ever. My cousin whom I told everything about my Saba rushed in the next morning and gave me a very tight hug and started crying.

I too had some tears in my eyes but managed to wielded control over them.

What happened dude this is how life turns around. I said to console him.

Nothing, He said.

I will show you something which would take your sadness off, I promise. I said.

It will not go.

Oh! My dear be calm and see what I am going to do, going behind the bars was perhaps the part of my life and please don't be sad now.

I cannot see your sufferings; your future is full of clouds.

Oh! My dear don't talk like this, this time I will make her my wife, I love her very much.

Don't make me emotional any more, he hugged me and cried.

See, I showed him the ring, tell me frankly how beautiful my Saba would look when I would put it into her finger? I think we are perfect matches, yeah? Tell anything dude why are you mum?

My dear Sam, Saba is no more yours.

What? What happened to my Saba, I said while grabbing him from his shoulders to move him to and fro.

This one year proved life taking for you, she got married!
What?

Yeah! She got married twice!

What are you saying? I couldn't believe if I am surviving any more.

Yeah! My dear Sam, besides this she has no one to look after, she is struggling for her life.

Where is she?

She is in her home, she got divorced twice she is still waiting you to come.

What divorced and what married? Open your mind and say it frankly, I said when my body was totally shivering.

I am correct my dear, her parents married her six months before to a shopkeeper and she divorced her husband the same day after giving a letter that she loves you. Her parents went hard at her and was forcefully remarried to such a person who was mentally sick where from she came back the next day after writing a note titled "*I am made for my Sam, the only man who can touch me*", in which she told everything to her husband. You must go and save her life now, you can't wait for your parents' decision. He told while hugging me once more strongly when emotions flew around.

I don't know where I stood after hearing those lines from him. My breathing got heavier, my heart beats faster and whole of my body was getting electric shocks. These words went inside to upshot even the boon marrow it looked if I would fell down and die. I couldn't see any more the world for me became darker. I turned into a statue without moving or saying anything. My mouth turned dry. The only solution was to go and make her my own forever, the family who married her with a shopkeeper would be quiet surprised and delighted to see me approaching them to seek her hand be given in mine for centuries. I reached her home ringed at the main entrance gate as a little child came out to open the door.

Hi, little angel, I wished her with emotions and tears running down.

"*Uncla, uncla, yet ha chene kahai, tiem che saalie gemit hashpatalash manj sab didi niesh, ehh hha eeh mummy te gemich bey gumut pap tey, tomov loyekhna sab didi wie path kolun sab didi tuetah balay doodh bey aaw tas aeskin tuetah khoon, taway che tiem gemit…near gass chiet*" she told me the saddest lines ever in the local language that "uncle, uncle, there is no one inside they have gone to the hospital because they assaulted and pounded Saba ferociously just now and large amount of blood came out from her mouth, she is serious…you also go there".

How could I stay there to tell anything more? I rushed to the hospital with my broken knees and found her lying in the emergency ward three surrounded by her parents and relatives.

I went in to hug her and tears rushed from my eyes, she was laid chest upwards with her eyes closed and confused hair, the doctors were treating her and everyone looked very upset and hurry, her face was totally blooded both of her legs were masked with bandages her arms and whole of her body had swelled everyone was stunned to see a stranger coming and hugging her like her family member. They gave me a flabbergasted look and could hear someone asking who I was. I looked deep into her eyes; I am here to marry you my *Ghaashu* I said helping her bemused hair to sit correct. But her eyes were still closed. What has happened to you my *Jaanu?* I said running my hand over her face.

I could see her trying to open her eyes to see me, yeah! My *Ghaashu*, I am here for you forever please look I have come, please talk to me my *Ghaashu*.

Her eyes run tears to her ears both sides, she got surprised seeing me besides her and tried to stand up but couldn't.

Jaanu, there is nothing in me for you to love, I am dying, I can only pray a daughter should never get birth to such parents. My *Jaanu*, I don't want you to survive, I know I will die before you now. I am paining inside hard, she told after placing her hand on the left side of my head to get my hair and neck brushed.

She wasn't able to speak clearly, her eyes rolled and she was unable to balance her neck even the swelling was going up the doctors were shouting that her blood level has gone very low due to the immense blood loss and it is an emergency case.

I could hear the doctors saying to her father that the pH level of her body has increased very much and the urine output is negligible.

I stood up to talk to the doctor. I got these were the symptoms of a kidney failure.

Hello, I am Sam, husband of that patient, pointing towards my Saba.

Yeah! I am a Nephrologist, Jahangeer rehman.

You please tell me her problem. I said.

I am sorry to say she is very serious, she is a victim of three main problems, first she is immensely depressed and that is a normal case, second she has been widely and continuously pounded on her back and abdomen as the result both of her kidneys had burst and bruised badly the symptoms are very severe and she needs transplantation of at least one kidney to survive much immediately. And third she needs blood to survive.

The sentence of the doctor gets my heart trodden. My mouth refused to say anything to the doctor, I remained dumb and my eyes burst into tears. Doctor, you don't bother I will donate both of these to her; I said with loud cries and even the doctors got very emotional.

I have made this announcement much earlier after diagnosing her problem but the people around are silently waiting for her death, you need to take steps hurry.

I was taken to a room before I was asked about my blood group any drug consumption or any disease and was asked to sit in an arm chair before the big blood sucking needle found its way deep into my veins.

After some minutes the doctors pulled the giant needle out and bandaged my arm. My Saba had to undergo a surgery, to maintain the blood level the doctors decide to transfuse whole blood into her.

Sir you please do fast, I told them about the kidney donation.

No, we cannot operate you before at least one day it is highly dangerous.

I want it right now; I can, it's the question of her life. I said and forced them to operate me fast.

The nurse came and told me that my Saba wanted to talk me. I was happy.

I went to sit beside her, and kissed her forehead.

My *Jaanu,* what had happened to me, she said.

Since my eyes were full of tears, she lifted her swollen had to wipe out my tears, I cried and hugged her once more.

Why are you crying, her voice wasn't clear she struggled to say.

You are ok, my *Ghaashu,* there is some minor depression, I had told you not to miss me so much, I said while touching her cheeks.

You were in jail and I was restless to get you back, she pulled my hand and kissed it.

You were missing me very much that is why you had got some depression, I didn't told her what had actually happened to her.

She struggled, and started in very low voice, then why my abdomen is paining so much.

You have some minor injuries on your abdomen that's why, you will get fine son and we shall get married to start our new life.

She again kissed my hand, and said "I love you *Jaanu*"

I love you too, I cried again.

I looked to the doctor who gestured it was getting late.

My heart never wanted to leave her that time but it was emergence. Ok, my *Ghaashu,* I will be here in some minutes, ok? I said while holding her arm.

Where are you going sit with me, I want you this time, don't leave me. Her voice went even low.

No, I have to bring some medicine for you, but she never knew her *Jaanu* was going to lose an organ but I was happy it was for her. She hold my hand but the doctors pulled me saying it's too late, I wanted to talk her for longer times but it was the question of her life.

Ok, *Ghaashu*, you just be calm I will be coming; I said with tears into my eyes.

Ok, my *Jaanu,* bring some fried chicken for me, today I will show you that I am not any less meat eater than you.

Ok, my *Ghaashu*, I looked into her eyes and managed some smile when the tears were simply unstoppable, my life, my Ghaashu, I will, I kissed her in pains and left for the operation theater.

The doctors gave me some documents to sign on and took me to the operation theater. It was the first operation of my life and I was feeling proud that it was for Saba who will be healthy soon. The team of doctors got in before wearing the green dress and masks and I laid down on the bed after removing my shirt. My mind was full of the past memories and thoughts, and how our life turned into slum. I start thinking about our future. I start thinking I have to fulfill many of her dreams. But my mind struck she would be waiting for the chicken she had demanded. I requested the doctor to tell the nurse to get some fried chicken for my Saba and he did. The doctors were getting ready, the medicines and the operation tools were standing on the table, I wasn't threatened to see the tools as I know them already. I put this thought away and started thinking about my Saba again.

Meanwhile someone knocked the door. It was the nurse; she called the senior doctor out.

After a minute he came in and asked me:----Sam, my son you put on your shirt, the operation is not needed now.

I thought there was some good news for my Saba may be there is a positive sign from her after talking to me, sir, why, is my Saba getting better? Has she shown some positive signs? I said feeling myself on the seventh sky with delight. I said while putting on the shirt.

No, my dear son, it's not like that he put his head down.

Then what happened, I said.

My dear son, I am sorry, your Saba is no more. He said and placed his hand over my head.

I stared into his eyes for some minutes with my veins coming out of my body. The flesh on my bones seems falling. I rushed to her and run my right hand over her face to get her mouth and eyes closed forever. I cried as loud as I could and got my clothes torn by punching my chest and slapping my head continuously, I start punching my abdomen to burst my kidneys which couldn't save her life. I kissed on her forehead with my tears running down her beautiful eyes which went away from me for lifetime. I looked into her beautiful face thinking what happened with me. I hate myself who cannot save her life, she only needed those things I had but still I couldn't do anything for her. I wanted to pull out both of my kidneys; my life became worthless and hollow. Everyone goes empty handed but she is the first person who went away forever with three things of mine that is my happiness, joy and my prosperity and gave me tears in return. I hold her hand and I felt if we were still going through the landscapes of Gulmarag. I saw a paper in her hand I pulled it out and kept it with me. Life belongs to one it belongs only to those who live and let others live. My life was shattered and there is no one mine in this miserable world. Millions of people love millions others but she was one who loved me millions of ways. I remembered her promises and one of them was "I want to die before you"

I went to my home and buried my face into my palms thinking what happened to us at last, I opened the letter I found in her hand after she left me here to die millions of times a day.

My jaanu.

You lost and I won. I had told you I will win this battle, I got my wish fulfilled and it is a dream come true for me. The world would never understand our love that is why I went afar from you but you are always in my heart, the people never allowed us to get married here, please don't cry I am there in your heart and I am waiting you in the heavens to become your bride forever. I never bowed in front of them neither anyone stopped me from loving you nor will anyone till the universe exists. I am waiting you in the heavens, I had never thought our life would turn such worse, it will be the first time in the history of love that we would be living in two different worlds apart from each other but loving much then we loved earlier. They did what they wanted now it is our turn to make the history. I believe our love never ends here I swear we would meet. We were born here only to come closer to each other we would get married in heavens. I know love is a small word but no one had described its meaning fully. You are my Jaan, my life, I am made for you. I am waiting. Love you very much.

Yours stupid Saba

Since then I am living with her letters, I am burst inside and want to die to meet my sweetheart.

I could see lots of tears into farad's eyes, he wept for me but I boosted and gave him confidence not to do such things which could make the condition of his beloved even worse. Her mom also heard this story and I got him married with her beloved very happily.

People are born to prepare themselves for death but I am an exception who is born to die millions of times a day, I will be born when I will finally die. *******